AT THE END OF THE DAY

SELECTED POEMS AND AN INTRODUCTORY ESSAY

Other Books by Phillip Lopate

POETRY

The Eyes Don't Always Want to Stay Open
The Daily Round

NONFICTION

Being With Children
Bachelorhood
Against Joie de Vivre
Portrait of My Body
Getting Personal: Selected Writings
Rudy Burckhardt, Photographer
Notes on Sontag
Totally Tenderly Tragically
Waterfront

FICTION

Confessions of Summer
The Rug Merchant
Two Marriages

ANTHOLOGIES

The Art of the Personal Essay
Writing New York
American Movie Critics
Journal of a Living Experiment

CONTENTS

AT THE END OF THE DAY

SELECTED POEMS AND AN INTRODUCTORY ESSAY

The Poetry Years

Though I am known today mostly as an essayist, occasionally as a fiction writer, for about fifteen years I wrote poetry. I published poems in countless little magazines, gave readings all over, earned a living of sorts as a poet in the schools, teaching the art to children, and put out two collections: the first in 1972, the second in 1976. When I look back at those years during which poetry formed such an important part of my identity, I am tempted to rub my eyes, as though recalling a time when I ran off and joined the circus; yet at the time it seemed a logical enough pursuit.

How had I started writing poetry in the first place? I can honestly say I had no ambitions to be a poet when I was younger. True, in elementary school I was by default the class poet, just as there was a boy who drew horses well and another boy who ran the fastest at Field Day. When Thanksgiving approached, I would be expected to craft a few stanzas about the pilgrims' feast. In junior high I wrote several tortured poems under the influence of the Beats. But by high school I had forsaken poetry for prose: if I had any literary ambitions, it was to be a novelist.

In college, joining the literary circle around *Columbia Review*, I befriended a number of emerging poets, including Jonathan Cott and Ron Padgett. Jonathan was my best friend and was highly cultivated, drawn to such serious, demanding authors as Holderlin, Lowell, Roethke. The Oklahoma-born Padgett and I had heard of each other before ever meeting, circling each other like gunfighters; he had even put the word out that he was going to break my butt. I, having hailed from the streets of Brooklyn, let it be known cockily that he was welcome to try. Of course when we finally met the conversation was amicable and respectful; he showed me a brilliant paper he had written about Pound and the medieval troubadours. Padgett had precociously started a poetry magazine back in high school, writing to poets he admired for contributions; and he came to New York to attend Columbia as part of a Tulsa émigré gang (which included Ted Berrigan, Joe Brainard, Dick Gallup) who affixed themselves immediately to the New York School of Poetry. The magnificent comic poet Kenneth Koch was the Pied Piper who had lured Padgett and others to Columbia, where Koch taught in the English Department. I attended the lunchtime readings Koch gave of his own poetry, and a memorable one of 19th Century Bad Poetry, which he delivered with robust oratory, cracking up every so often. Koch embodied what seemed to me at the time a zany poetics that incorporated Donald Duck, mock-epic parodies and neo-Dada game structures. I would later come to revere him as one of the most reflective, wide-ranging poets of our era, and in the last ten years of his life we became friends; but as an undergraduate I was too intimidated to take a course from him. So I settled for becoming a hanger-on in the New York School of Poetry scene, with entrée provided by Ron Padgett, all of us worshipping at the shrine of Koch, Frank O'Hara and John Ashbery.

The one whose poetry appealed to me most in that period was O'Hara, partly because of his unapologetically urban, movie-mad sensibility, partly because of his doctrine of Personalism. His example gave casual permission to construct a poem out of anything at hand, from a friend's remark to a movie star's collapse to a headline or honking car or sudden mood change.

Just as there was a *politique des auteurs* among film buffs, so a sort of *politque des poètes* existed, with battle lines drawn between the more Establishment-respected and prize-winning poets of the day, such as Robert Lowell, Richard Wilbur, John Berryman, Elizabeth Bishop, Richard Eberhart, Anthony Hecht, Anne Sexton, and so on, and the New York School, who drew their inspiration from the French modernist poets and the painting of Willem de Kooning, Jackson Pollock, Larry Rivers, Jane Freilicher, etc. Koch's poem "Fresh Air" was a manifesto against everything solemn, high-minded, ethically worrying— "academic," in a word—and called for a poetics of sensuous, experimental linguistic play. Of course these divisions grew fuzzier the closer you examined the matter: Koch himself taught in the academy, as Ashbery later would, and who could be wittier or more linguistically playful than Wilbur? But there was still this seeming antagonism between opposing teams, the one (the "established" poets) using poetry as a criticism of life, the other (the New York School) as a celebration of art. I remember visiting second-generation New York School poet Ted Berrigan in his East Village pad, and being told by him that he never mixed life with art. Art came from art, he said, not life. Anyone reading Ted's heart-breaking, autobiographical *Sonnets* would be hard-pressed to concur with his assertion; but that was at least the party line.

When I first began dipping into the poetry of Berryman, Lowell, Bishop, Sexton and Sylvia Plath, I felt guilty, like a Catholic reading books on the Index, and even guiltier for liking them so much. Lowell's *Life Studies* was a revelation for me; Berryman's *Dream Songs* and (much later) *Love & Fame* a grim delight. Surely it was possible to like both anguished confessional and breezy diaristic poetry? But I kept my taste for the former under wraps.

I remember attending a brilliant reading by Ashbery at NYU, when he premiered some of the poems from *Rivers and Mountains*. Perhaps trying to distance himself from the oracular, baton-beating style of Robert Duncan or the shamanistic intoning of Allen Ginsberg, Ashbery read his own poems with a curious ironic disdain, as if he had just bent down and picked up a piece of paper that had some improbable gibberish written on it. I hung around long enough to get invited to the cocktail party afterwards. At parties after New York School poetry readings, you would receive your literary marching orders. Reading tips were offered within an acceptably avant-garde framework that included such writers as Gertrude Stein, William S. Burroughs, Ronald Firbank…I remember talking to Ashbery after the reading: he recommended De Chirico's *Hebdomeros* and Raymond Roussel's *Impressions of Africa*, both hieratic texts in a Surrealist vein. On other occasions he might steer you to a set of unsung poets such as F. T. Prince, John Wheelwright and David Schubert. I always suspected he was throwing acolytes off the scent, and that he himself had been more deeply influenced by Wordsworth and Auden.

Myself, I could not get enough of *Rivers and Mountains*, and read it until the spine cracked. Later, after I began writing poetry, I spend a fruitless summer trying to imitate Ashbery's weary, elegant opacity. (No one could have shown less aptitude to write like John Ashbery than I, given my penchant for straightforward transparency; but he was *the* most influential poet of the period, and so I had to give it a try at least.)

In the last analysis, what I took from my days as a New York Poetry School fellow-traveler was less aesthetic than social. I had the privilege to watch the way a lively poetry scene mushroomed at St. Marks' Church on the Bouwerie, in the East Village, under the nurturance of Anne Waldman. This was the closest I would ever come to the Banquet Years, and though I have always considered myself a literary loner, it gave me a glimpse of how a circle, a generation, a movement, a bohemia functioned. I accepted the poets' generous invitations to parties, to passed joints, to publications in mimeo magazines, to friendships and acquaintanceships. What they made of me I have no idea. My first wife Carol and I lived way uptown, at the northern end of Manhattan above the Cloisters: one time we threw a party and invited the St. Mark's crowd to it, though they seemed wary ever of venturing above 14th Street. They arrived late, having brought with them on the A train enough reading matter for an ocean crossing, and immediately headed for the bedroom to get stoned, ignoring my other literary friends in the living room. But if the St. Marks poets were insular, they were also warmly loyal. I was fascinated by the way they supported each other. I once asked Ron Padgett how he and Ted Berrigan critiqued one another's poems. "I just say, 'That's totally terrific, Ted,' and when I show him mine he says 'That's totally terrific' to me." Whether this was actually true I have my doubts, but the lesson seemed to be that critical fussiness was passé. Another time I was visiting the poet (and future art critic) Peter Schjeldahl in his apartment, and I commented with surprise that he kept a top 40 rock station on all the time. What did he do when bad songs came on the air? Schjeldahl said obstinately, "There are no bad rock songs today." Was he pulling my leg, or did he really believe that? I felt like a visitor from the 19th Century.

I also watched with surprise and maybe envy how the poets

and their wives (or husbands) swapped partners. Ted Berrigan read a poem at St. Mark's Church that went something like: "When you sleep with your best friend's wife/ She gets fucked/ He gets fucked/ And you get fucked." Loud titters from the cognoscenti, who knew the poem's other referents, both present in the audience that night.

As eye-opening as all this was, it did not necessarily make me want to be a poet. That came about another way.

Living on the brink of poverty, I was looking for some freelance editorial work (often a euphemism for ghostwriting, which I did extensively during this period), when I came upon a notice requesting readers to help edit a new poetry anthology. Reading was one thing I felt sure I could do; I did very little else. So I answered the ad and was summoned to a noon interview at the home of one Hy Sobiloff.

Mr. Sobiloff, often referred to in those days as "the businessman-poet," was a wealthy investor and venture capitalist who lived in a very tony townhouse on East 77th Street in the Upper East Side. He had several servants, and his townhouse had its own elevator, which impressed the hell out of me. A Chinese houseboy answered the door, brought me into the parlor and told me to wait, as Mr. Sobiloff was just getting up. I had time to examine the antiques and indifferent paintings before the great man himself appeared, in a silk striped robe: his fleshy, curt, bald-headed, imperial manner put me instantly in mind of Louis Calhern in *The Asphalt Jungle*, some sort of mobster kingpin or political boss (Calhern also played the title role in *Julius Caesar*). Sobiloff explained the nature of the project, which was to revise the immensely popular poetry anthologies that had been edited by his late friend Oscar Williams. I was happy to tell him that my own mother had read aloud from them to us as children such favorites as Alfred Noyes' "The Highwayman." Poetically, you might say, Oscar Williams' anthologies were mother's-milk to me. Sobiloff gruffly cut me off, saying the point was that they needed to be updated. He had undertaken the chore as an act of devotion to a friend who'd passed away. He pointed to several precipitously tall stacks of poetry books on French Empire chairs and said, "I know all this stuff cold but I can't be bothered to go through 'em. I'm too busy. That's why I need an assistant." Somehow I doubted he was as familiar with the contents of these volumes as he pretended, but I played along, familiar as I was with my ghostwriting clients' need to pretend omniscience. On my end, I bluffed like crazy about my knowledge of poetry. The interview lasted ten minutes at most. He seemed satisfied; we agreed on a salary, and I took away a few shopping bags full of books.

I had now to educate myself as quickly as possible in the English and American poetic canon. I was overwhelmed by the vast amounts of poetry I would have to absorb, but I began by plowing through the original Williams anthologies. I quickly saw that Oscar Williams had put his friend Hy in the books, as he had his wife Gene Derwood and himself, though their verse hardly seemed in the same league with Keats and Whitman. Sobiloff, I learned, was philanthropically active, and a heavy supporter of poetry societies and magazines. I was too shy to ask Sobiloff how he had made his millions, but someone in the know told me that he had started in the furniture business, and had perfected a scheme of buying a second, failing business and transferring all the assets from the first business to the second; then shutting that down, and transferring all the assets of the second to a third failing business…in any case, some kind of fiscal legerdemain.

Shortly after beginning the job I learned I was not the only poetry reader; Sobiloff had hired two others, like a gambler placing bets across the board. At first he kept us strictly separate; but in time I was able to contact them, and consolidate my position as First Reader, primer ante pares, by offering to coordinate the project for a slightly higher fee. He appreciated my ruthlessness, I think. It was Sobiloff who said once in passing that he was flying off on vacation to the Bahamas, leaving the city because he "was tired of all those ghetto faces," a statement so shocking and appalling to me that I was almost charmed by its brazenness. In any case I never forgot it. I myself came from the ghetto and wondered when he would ferret this fact out. On another visit to the boss I met a lady friend of his whom I took to be his mistress, a woman in her fifties with the body of an ex-showgirl and a face that looked hard and cunning, to say the least. When Sobiloff left the room for a minute she warned me not to take advantage of her Hy, if I knew what was good for me.

Believe me, I had no intention of cutting corners. My work schedule consisted of reading four poetry books a day minimum. Most of them came from the library, some from used book stores—our boss had given us permission to augment his limited stock, and I saved the receipts for him. I would wake up and eat breakfast while starting on the first, get dressed, finish reading the book, take some notes about possible selections and go off for a walk with a bag lunch around noontime, often ending on a bench in Riverside Park (my wife and I had by this time moved down from Inwood to West 104th Street, near Columbia), where I would read a second book and begin paging through a third…By now I was starting to feel headachy from eye-strain and nauseous from a surfeit of poetic expressiveness, so I would give it a rest, then turn to book four in the late afternoon, and maybe book five that evening, if I had anything left in me. I recommend this brutal pedagogic method of saturation reading to anyone with literary ambitions. Over-stuffed like a goose for the manufacture of *foie gras*, I had no choice but to secrete my own poems. So mentally swamped with the elevated lyrical language of others, out of sheer defensive survival I needed to have my say.

Two other factors, besides the anthology reader gig, sparked my entry into poetry in the years I am describing, 1967–69: the political upheaval of the anti-war movement and the breakdown of my marriage. They were not unrelated. Living as we did fairly close to Columbia University, I got swept up in the 1968 student revolt and reentered my old Alma Mater as a trouble-making alumnus. Just as I had been a hanger-on at the New York School of Poetry scene, so now I became a fellow-traveler of the New Left, participating in demonstrations, political meetings and study groups, reading Marxist texts along with all the poetry. I never felt entirely comfortable with the posture of radicalism, nor could I embrace deep-down the hope of making revolution, being an ex-scholarship kid from the ghetto still trying to claw my way into the middle class. But the heady Sixties talk of sexual liberation and down with the bourgeoisie and smashing monogamy had a destabilizing effect on my domestic arrangements. Not that I can blame the failure of that first marriage on the revolutionary Left! I had married too young, at twenty, and hadn't a clue; we both made mistakes, which I needn't go into here.

Meanwhile, my first novel had not found a publisher; I was unable to take defeat in stride and start on a second one. Writing novels requires a calm, settled, bourgeois existence, and the pay-off is deferred for years. The fragmentation I felt so painfully in those days would not permit me to submerge myself again in a prolonged alternate dream-narrative: I was too antsy, too much at the mercy of day-to-day reality. I needed a form I could turn to with quicker results, snatching a few hours here and there from a patched-together free-lance existence and the emotional confusion of whether to leave or stay. Hence, poetry.

My first poems seemed to emerge from conjugal dilemma. I still hoped we could salvage the marriage, if we both behaved responsibly and maturely. (Yeah, right.) These poems now strike me as tentative and hypocritical, the way a couple in their last stage bullshits during marriage counseling while secretly eyeing the exit. Formally, I was feeling my way into poetry at the same time I was feeling my way out of the marriage. By the time our marriage had definitively collapsed, I was on much firmer ground. Incidentally, I have always derived poetic inspiration from break-ups. The rejection of love produces an emotional clarity in me, while the return to solitude arouses a need to solace myself with lyrical resignation—either that or revenge.

I had decided to leave Carol and New York for California, the promised land of youth culture. Before I decamped, I turned in my lists of recommendations for the updated anthologies. It's funny to recall what I thought in my youthful exuberance would make for such substantial improvements. I had wanted the collections to seem less stuffy, less "academic," so I added Bessie Smith and Bob Dylan lyrics, and Native American chants, and a slew of Black poets, and of course increased the selections of the New

York School poets, and F. T. Prince, John Wheelwright, Robert Creeley, George Oppen, Ed Dorn and Allen Ginsberg, among others. Sobiloff looked them over without a word. Years later, when the revised anthologies appeared, I had a hard time finding any evidence of my labors. But the job had served its purpose: it had given me a condensed poetic education.

The poets who influenced me the most at the beginning of my poetic career were William Carlos Williams, Frank O'Hara, Pablo Neruda, Vladimir Mayakovsky, and Randall Jarrell. I was happy to purloin Williams' three-line stanzas or O'Hara's splattering of words across the page; to imitate Mayakovsky's mock-megalomaniac outbursts, Neruda's surreal inventories or the loquacity of late Jarrell. Later on I would fall in love with the dramatic monologues at the back of Pasternak's *Doctor Zhivago*, and Cavafy's deceptively simple lyrics and history poems, and Pavese's *Hard Labor*, with its dense materialist details of quotidian working-class life.

I was searching for something that made me happy whenever I found it, but I still didn't know how to characterize it. Though I had been a fan of Neruda's, when I attended a reading of his at the 92nd Street Y he put me off with his hammy, Stalin Prize delivery. It was another Chilean poet, Nicanor Parra, who crystallized for me what I was looking for, with his collection *Poems and Anti-Poems*. This taste for "anti-poetry," for grubby reality, is addressed by Wallace Stevens in his preface to the 1934 *Collected Poems* by William Carlos Williams, when he describes Williams as someone for whom "the anti-poetic is that truth, that reality to which all of us are forever fleeing." I was drawn to the anti-poetic for a number of reasons. First, my training had been in fiction, and I was still very charmed by the sound of conversational prose. Though literary critics might disparage a poem as being "chopped-up prose," that was insufficient to condemn it in my eyes. Quite the contrary: it interested me, perversely, to see how far one could go in that direction and still get away with it. I also found it attractive when poets employed a complex syntax that took a whole stanza or sonnet to uncoil—more so than a row of staccato end-stopped lines. A storyteller at heart, I continued to like narrative. Some of Parra's and Cavafy's narrative situations were like little short stories: a room, a memory, a pickup.

Second, I was much more intrigued by poetic statement than by metaphor, simile and image. When I heard it said that great poets were characterized by their gift for metaphor, it rankled me. I did not go out of my way to find metaphors; if an apt one swam into my brain while I was writing a poem, I put it in; if not, not. A profusion of metaphor and simile seemed to me, at this point, forced. I even developed a theory that the late manner of certain poets, such as Pasternak and Montale, favored unadorned poetic statement, because they no longer felt the need to show off with metaphors to prove their poetic bona fides.

Third, I was rebelling against the lingering idea that poems should contain words or emotions that were suitably "poetic"— the beauties of nature, flowers, finches, rapture, elevated sentiment; I was drawn to a more sardonic poetry that would traffic in mundane commercial objects, business terms, legalese, you name it. It pleased me beyond measure to be able to use a word like "bicameral" in a poem on Allende. A city rat, I had no command of the names of flora and fauna, and needed to stake my claim with vocabulary that would verge on the prosaic and anti-romantic.

Finally, being poetically self-taught and, despite having read books on prosody from Saintsbury to Hollander, finding that very little of it stuck to me, never able to master my quantities, meters and values, never having gone to graduate school to study poetry, I still composed poems largely intuitively, on the basis of what rhythms or combinations "sounded right" to my ear. This awkward situation made me feel at a disadvantage among trained poets. But it also drove me to embrace the anti-poetic tradition that ran like a heretical streak through poetic history. Essentially I was trying to turn a limitation (my ignorance) into a strength (my preference for the anti-poetic).

To some degree, I was taking permission from the era's looser standards. The 1960s allowed for a wide open, pluralistic (some would say amateurish) poetics. The ascendance of the oral, first-word-best-word "rap" through the Beats and black activist poets such as Gil Scott Heron and the Last Poets, the cultural enthronement of rock troubadours, the proliferation of open readings and mimeo magazines, the promotion of children's poetry and ethnopoetics, all contributed to the idea that anyone could write poetry, or had the right to call oneself a poet; you didn't need a credential. It may have been an invitation to charlatanism and self-delusion, but it also made for a no-holds- barred, anything-goes sense of freedom; and I suppose I sneaked in under that umbrella.

A key determinant for me during these years was becoming friends with the poet Bill Zavatsky, a friendship I am happy to say has lasted forty years. Zavatsky is a large-hearted, open, funny man and a very fine poet, as well as a capable jazz pianist. When I first met him around 1968 he was writing ebullient verse that ran arpeggios in all directions. His verbal fireworks showed the influence of the French Surrealists, particularly Andre Bréton, whom he later translated. At the same time, he was trying to master a leaner lyric with more sincerity and humanity, to put more honest emotions, situations and characters into his poems. Robert Lowell once commented that he found it hard to "people" his poems. I, with my fiction background and interest in psychological cul-de-sacs, found that part relatively easy; my poetic struggles were on another plane. In any case, Zavatsky was drawn to what I was doing, and he encouraged me to keep writing situational, reality-based poems.

Zavatsky had recently gotten an MFA in poetry-writing at Columbia, where he'd studied with Stanley Kunitz and Harvey Shapiro, and he introduced me to a circle of young Kunitz/Shapiro-trained poets, which included Hugh Seidman, Mark Rudman and Louise Gluck, who hung out at the West End Bar and other venues in Morningside Heights. Soon I was participating in their open readings, and learning from them. Through them I became familiar with another poetic model, the Objectivists (George Oppen, Louis Zukofsky and Carl Rakosi), and their younger allies, Harvey Shapiro, Armand Schwerner and David Ignatow. I was particularly taken with the hard-bitten, wry, tight urban lyrics of Shapiro and Ignatow. Certain of my poems seem to have come directly out of an attempt to write like them.

But the poet in the Objectivist orbit who came to affect me most was Charles Reznikoff. He was still around then, though elderly, and had been rediscovered, championed by younger poets, who were as moved by his example of humility and non-careerism as by his spare, tender poems. Reznikoff had for years published his own verse, gone his own solitary way. He had fashioned a poetics of daily observation and reflection, taking long walks and then drafting his urban encounters into concise accounts in verse. His poems eschewed all verbal razzle-dazzle, yet they shimmered with a sympathy and humanity which never sentimentalized, including as they did the recognition of human cruelty. In person and on the page, he had a quality of resignation or acceptance (which was it? both, perhaps) that suggested spiritual wisdom. And no one was more exposed to the charge of being prosaic or "anti-poetic." His long-lined autobiographical sequence, "Early History of a Writer," reads stubbornly close to chopped-up prose—an engrossing personal essay with a ragged right-hand margin. What made him, in the end, truly poetic was his economical use of language and his limpid vision of reality, which might be compared to Basho and Li Po.

Reznikoff provided a solution to my guilt about not being able to achieve the proper (meaning, MFA-approved) poetic surface: I had only to write down what I saw, heard and thought, as honestly as possible, and the poetry would take care of itself. The problem was that I could never be as pure a being as Reznikoff; and some of my attempts to write like him misfired from disingenuous over-simplicity. I also had an incurable taste for the ironic-rationalizing or mischievously analytical narrator, which led me in distinctly non-Reznikoffian directions (see, for instance, "Just to Spoil Everything" and "The Japanophiles"). But Reznikoff was never far off, once I had admitted him into my pantheon as a benign conscience, a figure of enduring through failure.

Two other, nonliterary influences on my poetry during that time deserve mention. The first was psychotherapy. I was seeing a Jungian psychologist named George Romney, a Cuban émigré who smoked cigarillos and had wavy black hair and an infectious laugh; it became my secret goal to provoke that laugh of his as often as possible in sessions. I would tell him about my experiences, and sometimes in the midst of relating them they would cohere into a kind of improvised poem, which would make him chuckle and which I would then go home and try to write down. In this way my long poem "The Blue Pants" came about. George also frequently asked me, as therapists are wont to do, what I was feeling in the moment, directing my attention to the emotion physiologically manifesting and gurgling in my body. Out of this practice of attempting to pin down emotional states came poems such as "Numbness," "Not Sadness Which Is Always There," and "Clearing a Space." The very ambition to write poems based in the present moment—to open myself to the here-and-now, as it were—derived from techniques I had been learning in psychotherapy.

The second crucial nonliterary influence on my poetry was teaching inner-city children and teenagers. I worked as a poet-in-the-schools for over a dozen years, first helping high school dropouts in East Harlem get their equivalency degree, then directing a program for Teachers & Writers Collaborative at P.S. 75 in the Upper West Side of Manhattan. Poems such as "Satin Doll" and "Rumors" (along with my first published prose book, *Being With Children*), resulted from that work experience, which brought me closer to my own memories of childhood and early adolescence.

Teaching kids grew partly out of a desire to be socially useful: to put my politics into practice. I was also looking for ways to incorporate my politics into my poetry. In one case, I had been leafing through a picture book of Cuban revolutionary art, and I came upon a propaganda poster with the title "Solidarity with Mozambique," and wondered how on earth I could ever feel my way into bonding with a struggle that seemed so far away and so abstract. I began writing about daily occurrences in New York City, then tried to reach, by concentric circles leading farther and farther away from myself, the rebels in Mozambique. (Not that I ever convincingly made it.) My poem "Allende" required no such elaborate device: I was simply shaken by the overthrow of the Chilean leftist's government and wanted to register my dismay and disenchanted skepticism without resorting to the usual consoling *Venceremos* clichés.

Finally, I took scraps from everything around me and built a poetic nest with them: movie references ("Film Noir"), which were hard to resist, given my lifelong cinephilia; musical refrains (I kept playing Lotte Lenya's double album, and her rendition of "Lost in the Stars" undoubtedly seeped into my "Furnished Room"); the economic recession and New York City default scare of 1975 ("The Last Slow Days of Summer"); the exploding gentrification that followed, all round my apartment on West 71st Street ("Saturday on the West Side of Assisi"); phone conversations ("We Who Are Your Closest Friends"); the parade of failed romances and breakup scenes ("Hearts," "The Thrill of the First Night").

Around 1977, I started writing personal essays and also went back to longer fiction. I see in retrospect the way I was handling the same material, the same themes, in poetry and prose. "The Second Marriage" reads like a poem-précis of the novella by the same title. A protest against "the bullying urge to feel" can be found in "Numbness" and the essay "Against Joie de Vivre." "Secrets, Rehearsals" was like a dry run for my essay, "The Story of My Father." The single person learning to be alone is a theme sounded in many of these poems no less than in the prose that makes up my first essay collection, *Bachelorhood*.

Regardless of the genre I happened to working in, I found myself resisting the transcendent. I was skeptical of all triumphalism, both positive (redemption) and negative (apocalypse). I threw in my lot with ordinary life, "the daily round." This mistrust of transcendence was another way in which I felt myself out of step with the ideological presuppositions of much contemporary poetry. But again, I was trying to turn weakness into strength: the inability to reach the stars, to achieve anything like spiritual sublimity, became a stubborn claim that the earth is all we have—a brief for groundedness.

To go back to 1972: I had been amassing sufficient poems for a first collection when a printer based in Northampton approached me and offered to put them out in a chapbook. The plan was for me to spend the month of August at his print shop, learning to operate a letter press and assisting in the production of the book, to be entitled *The Eyes Don't Always Want to Stay Open*. When I arrived in Northampton, however, I discovered that the printer and his wife were going through a messy divorce, and he was temporarily closing the business while they sorted out the division of conjugal assets. I was welcome, he said, to stay in their house for the month of August, now that it had been vacated by both husband and wife, who had moved in with their new lovers. As I had no other plans for summer vacation, I decided to stick it out and explore the town and the surrounding Massachusetts countryside. I was miserably lonely, and felt foolish and hollow. But as it happened, an elderly woman neighbor, highly cultivated, befriended me. She knew how to operate the letter press. So we set in type exactly one of my poems, the paranoid epistle "We Who Are Your Closest Friends," as a broadside. (Anne Lamott, to my surprise, included this poem in her popular writing manual, *Bird by Bird*, thus bringing it to thousands of readers it would otherwise not have reached).

Returning to the city, discouraged that there would be no chapbook after all, I visited Bill Zavatsky and his wife Phyllis the first night back, hoping they might cheer me up. Zavatsky, who had already edited the poetry magazines *SUN* and *Roy Rogers*, had been mulling over the idea of someday starting his own small poetry press. Seeing me so disappointed he told me not to worry; he would put out my collection himself. To my astonished gratitude he began retyping the manuscript immediately, and he stayed up half the night finishing the job, while I slept (more or less) on his couch. In the morning he had a manuscript ready to put into production. Thus was born in 1972 the press called SUN, which would go on to publish books by Ron Padgett, Harvey Shapiro, Paul Violi, Raymond Roussel, Paul Auster and Zavatsky himself, among others, but whose maiden publication was *The Eyes Don't Always Want to Stay Open*. My second collection, *The Daily Round*, would follow, also from SUN, in 1976.

What remains to be told is how or why I gave up writing poetry. There is a simple answer and a complicated one. First the simple one:

In 1980 I moved to Houston, Texas, to teach in the University of Houston. I had been recruited as the creative writing program's first prose writer, on the basis of my memoir about teaching, *Being with Children*, my novel *Confessions of Summer* and my soon-to-be-released personal essay collection, *Bachelorhood*. If in New York I had been accepted as a poet, such was not the case in Houston. I was not permitted to teach poetry courses, in spite of having published two books' worth. I need not have taken it personally: my colleagues Rosellen Brown and Ntozake Shange, both of whom had written poetry books but were hired as prose writers, faced the same prohibition at that university.

A higher, "purer" standard of what it took to be a poet seemed to reign in that corner of academia, based partly on the possession of an MFA credential, and partly on the networking of the professional poetry world. I got a real taste of the way that poetry guild mentality operated: the mentoring and bestowal of the blessing on a chosen few acolytes, whose books would then be recommended for publication, and the whole priestly sense of the Poet as someone of rare vatic powers. The non-exclusionary ethos of the Sixties and early Seventies had ended, in the face of the writing program-generated mystique of technique. The impression was conveyed that there could only be two dozen poets at most in one era who had received the vision. I knew I'd never gotten a message from on high: I did not fit that bill. My sense of myself as a poet began to shrivel up.

But that simple explanation is false. It would be wrong to blame my colleagues for killing the urge, since anyone who can be discouraged so easily from writing poetry is not cut out to be a poet. The truth is that I had already begun moving away from poetry before I came down to Houston, having fallen in love with the personal essay and its possibilities. I found in the personal essay a wonderful plasticity, which combined the narrative, storytelling aspects of fiction with the lyrical, associative qualities of poetry. If, as Robert Bly recommended, American poets should learn to "leap" freely from line to line, from image to image and subject to subject, I realized I could do that as easily in the personal essay as in a poem. Moreover, I could never have been deterred from writing poetry if my Houston colleagues' judgment had not gibed with something already inside me, some insecure spot that made me feel that, on some level, I was an imposter. It had been a good long run, but it was time to stop pretending I was a poet.

Around 1983 I drifted away from writing poems, the only exceptions being the occasional birthday ode or the e-mail poems I would exchange with my daughter when I was away, to encourage her to send me her own poems. But recently, when offered the chance to have these two earlier collections reprinted, along with any additional poems that were not included in them, I found myself going through this material and—liking much of it. As I retyped individual poems in my computer, I would change phrases, sharpen a rhythm, clarify an idea. I remembered how much fun it was to write poems, how happily engaged I could be for hours in tiny adjustments. Suddenly I couldn't understand why I had given it up.

Will I take up the practice again? I certainly hope so. I'm well aware that established prose writers often publish their hobbyish poems out of vanity. I would like to think there is more going on here in this collection: the urge to give pleasure to new readers. When I read my old poems today, it strikes me with a mixture of regret and relief that I am no longer the person who wrote them. Some are obviously young man's poems, and their callow hungers embarrass me now. Yet I cannot help finding that younger self touching, and in any case, revealing. It is not for me, finally, to judge them as poems. I will leave that up to you.

—*Phillip Lopate*

PART 1
THE EYES DON'T ALWAYS WANT TO STAY OPEN

We Who Are Your Closest Friends

we who are
your closest friends
feel the time
has come to tell you
that every Thursday
we have been meeting
as a group
to devise ways
to keep you
in perpetual uncertainty
frustration
discontent and
torture
by neither loving you
as much as you want
nor cutting you adrift

your analyst is
in on it
plus your boyfriend
and your ex-husband
and we have pledged
to disappoint you
as long as you need us

in announcing our
association
we realize we have
placed in your hands
a possible antidote
against uncertainty
indeed against ourselves
but since our Thursday nights
have brought us

to a community of purpose
rare in itself
with you as
the natural center
we feel hopeful you
will continue to make
unreasonable
demands for affection
if not as a consequence
of your
disastrous personality

then for thc good of the collective

Snowball Journal

to Carol

1.

Our room, says the lady of the house
is nicer than one in a motel
                    and she's right
second-storey bay windows
a mushy double bed   T.V.
and sportsman and gun magazines

2.

We'll take it
But not the meal plan.

3.

It turns out she is an alcoholic

4.

Those circular curtain rods
are a nice personal touch
she must have put a lot of work
                    into this house…
we settle down to make love
on a chair
the dependable thrill of foreign rooms, positions
                    violating good people's rugs

5.

I stroke your legs and breasts as you straddle me

6.

We bring out the Polaroid
take pictures of our bodies relaxed
Just lean against the radiator, your back to the sun
a smile of bones dissolving
       I squeeze the knob until it says YES

7.

But you always manage
to take three more pictures of me
than I do of you

8.

We must take a stroll in the woods before the sun goes down
you slip out while I am reading
       and drive to the country store
       bringing back Vermont cheese,
       bread for sandwiches, Utica beer
       and Tasty Cups
       For this I love you

you even get undressed again
so we can both snack in bed
with the crumbs falling between us

9.

We'll never see Vermont this way
up and dressed for our 5 o'clock walk—
the hills above us make us laugh
they're all so pretty!
       and we don't laugh that easily

          with my arm around your waist

it seems child's play to live with you
breathe in the electric air
what has happened to all our demands
don't even think about them
     if you kiss my left ear lobe
     and lick the other one
     I'll be as happy as

10.

The sun is dying on the sharp points of the tree-tops
not just disappearing
soon we'll have to go back to the car, it's
getting cold

11.

I can't resist—I surprise you with a snowball
     The snow dribbles onto your
         bare breasts
now you have 'snowy breasts'

12.

Dinner is delicious! We compliment each other
for walking out of that expensive Auberge down the road
and saying no to The Reluctant Panther
This one is moderate but certainly as good as the others!
We listen with delight as people in the next room
     are being turned away

     Thank goodness we made our reservations just in time!

'Try the banana-loaf bread'
  'I can't believe these lamb chops!'
    greasing our teeth and fingers into the bone

Families of skiers clomp into the dining room
study menus, talking about the slopes
Most have fat asses and need the exercise
But they are ordering everything! lobster with roast beef
       and pie
What could be more fun than eating! they cry
a hearty meal after a long day outdoors
is justice.

    Mother and daughter look-alikes
    That girl could be pretty if she lost fifteen pounds
    Now you know what she'll be like at forty.

13.

At night you fall asleep
and I stay up to read
        nothing on television

14.

The next day—clouds, a little somber
we wake up leisurely
and dawdle over breakfast in the trucker's diner
     you seem apprehensive
while I play record after record on the jukebox
that morning you came into our room
I was stretched across the double-bed
"Guess what?" you announced—beaming, dramatic—
"I started my period."

    Now you're having second thoughts about it?

    Very well, an honest discussion
       let's take stock of our lives
       by all means, say

what's on your mind...
this too is part of vacations

15.

We have found a woods that is really private
Fresh-cut lumber, a carrot smell—
on the ground wood shavings, snow, pine cones
            and animal tracks (deer hooves)
I want to go where it's completely hooded
away from the trail
live like an animal between the spaces of trees

        you are afraid that the ice will crack
        you would go, you say, if you had better boots

        a difference of opinion

We sit cautiously on a pile of snow
What, are you shivering?
like a maniac I reach into your pants
                with chilling fingers
so that you will be warmer
                and you shudder
                at the cheap power I have over you
                to make you sigh

16.

The good mood regained

17.

Looking at the Green Mountains from a roadside promontory
Peru, Vermont—

The Woman Thinks:

This is a place to raise children
live correctly
come to peace with myself

The Man Thinks:

perfect landscape
of mountains, firs and snow
I toss a snowball into the purest fields
to see if this is a beauty that mars easily
or deserves my worship

18. *Coda*

When we were standing before the mountains
the sun leaking pools on the snowy fields
the hard quiet of the barn and the owner's house
the watchdog's bark
sky so intense we could only look through a crack in our lids
and yet everything was blue—

how little I've been able to take with me
back one week in the city

In the Time

In the time it takes to eat half an orange
close by on the night table
after making love to our heart's content
when the taste buds are aroused to an incredible pitch

In the time in the underground from Victoria to Earl's Court
Sunday morning on a visit to a friend
In the time from rapping on his basement window
to his slipping on an undershirt, pulling the lightswitch
passing a hand over his face and opening the door

In the time it takes to decide to leave someone
In the time it takes to actually leave her…

In the time one eats an apple
hurrying before the skinless meat turns brown
or the air bubbles settle in a glass of water

In the time that it takes a man to fix his dinner
In the time that it takes a woman to fix it

between the neighbor's apartment window and my window
between the neighbor's cat and my cat

In the time that it takes to open the door before the Negro
      doorman gets it
before he understands what I'm doing and reaches forward
      faster than me
and I drop my hand
smile, say Thank you
and in the time it takes to write out his check for Christmas
thinking all the while how I hate this tipping system
and thinking of the arguments for it

In the time that a post-industrial society wakens to the
        possibility of Revolution
and in the time it takes for that hope to evaporate
In the time that a writer pauses between lines, picking his
        teeth
and finally goes to the dictionary

In the time it takes for children to shoot up their hands

and then forget what they were going to say—
or for intuitive intellects to grasp the full meaning
and realize afterwards that they didn't

In the time that I used to walk you down to the river

and lie on your lap
and discuss the new morality
while headlights blinked in the bushes of the Jersey side

In just that time
In just that time
In just that time
would I take my life

White Sails

I dreamt I saw a newsreel of a funeral.
White banquet tables were sailing down the Vltava;
The barges slowly cleared the low stone bridges
Stubbing the water with their lightbulbs.

Ego! Ego! the crowd yelled out
As if the body of Adonis had passed by.
But all I could see were the stuffed cabbage
And glistening corn on the cob

Shivering against two blocks of ice.
Who is it? I asked the spectators
And without an answer I started to cry,
Because the camera was moving so quickly

Along the faces
Lining the banks in their medieval grief;
And nothing is more piercing than a tracking shot
Past millions stiff in devotion or helplessness.

I knew how they felt: in my stomach
Grainy, sealed tight with bottle caps,
Where there's so much weeping, and
Every funeral is a relief.

I started to sail after them; then
The lights went on.
Incredible, I thought—a miraculous document.
But as I turned
To share the audience's love,
I realized that no one else had gotten it
Except for one young woman, way toward the back,
Hair pinned up, a turquoise jumper,
Who kept blowing her nose into a wet kleenex.

"Wasn't that great?" I caught up to her.
She smiled agreement through the shreds of tissue
And I saw who it was, and we both burst into tears!

She Wishes She Had What She Has

She wishes she could be married to her husband
Her tits like fried eggs are burning for him at El Paso Airport
As he touches down she crosses her arms over her chest
To push back the sigh.
The married couple French-kisses, reminding him of the time
       she was sickly thin
And he had to support her in the terminal so that she would
      not faint.

She wishes that if she marries it will be to someone tall dark
and foreign-looking
From the inside of her Kansas vulva she dreams of a foreign-
      looking intellectual husband
She has one: he fits into the mythology of her desire
As he touches down he sweeps her off her feet
And into complications, wind tunnels, and no security
Other than that she has him to walk with in the streets of
      El Paso.

Still, she wishes that he would arrive soon
His plane is late, and she has been waiting all morning
Close to tears—closer to resentment
Which may turn into the reserved air that Phillip hates
When he expects his joyous greeting, all smiles, all tears,
      all tits
But how long can she hold this hard-on of expectation?

She wishes now that someone who is tall, dark, intellectual
      and foreign-looking will come into the lobby
And she will jump up and kiss him
No matter whether he is her husband or not, just so that he
      seems exactly like her husband
(And many men are like many other men, exactly alike)

And that this one will agree to take her for his wife
As the first one did, and even more than the first one did.
For otherwise, why this separation?

Edwardian Dilemmas

What's this prickling that I feel
        dragging me from a contented sleep?
Your pubic hairs grazing against my ass…
        What am I to make of your belly
nudging me in soft places when
        I had just been dreaming of Allen Ginsberg
sending me a letter, "Phil, I have
        no unused poems for the magazine,
but your stuff is
        terrific! I sincerely admire it,
keep me posted…" And I'm sure he had more
        to say but your lips exhaling on my back
seem different in a way that I,
        trained in the School for Husbands,
can read passing well: that you're
        awake and would like me to be also.

"What? What is it?" I say.
        "Just love," you whisper to yourself,
and: "I love my precious."
        Good; I pat your thigh, hoping
it's all right to take love passively,
        yawn, pull the covers around my head
and start swimming again toward Allen
        who is wearing a witch's hat for *Time,*
someone else's hero now…
        or to any happy vision
let me climb aboard, into the arms
        of naked girls in sailboats, kaleidoscopes

Meanwhile you blow your nose
        and kiss me (apologizing for the noise?
cuddling up? or wanting something?)
        In the name of love you are waking me up!

"What's the matter."
        "Phillip, my throat hurts."

"Mm... I'm sorry."
     "I really am sick this time..."
"Can I get you anything?"
     "Some orange juice?"
"All right." I sit up.
     I am starting to remember the overhanging
worries from teaching in a ghetto school
     to unpublished works to U.S. imperialism.
"Wait, you don't have to bring me orange juice
     it's too much trouble, you'll have to make it...
Just bring me an orange."—"No, I'll do it!"
     Am I so incompetent I can't open a can?

I fetch a bathrobe from the closet
     the cat tearing after me, rubbing
his head against my legs
     while I turn the automatic can opener.
Gusts of cold air blow through the window
     of our river-view apartment. The can is
crusted with ice, my hand frozen to the bottom
     as I scoop out the doughy orange compost
with a knife...It takes forever.
     I realize I am only doing
what you do for me every day.
     What pitiful meowing! and shivering barefoot
I decide that he too will be fed:
     All will receive food from my hands.

The Horny Couple

And sometimes in the evening
a dryness enters like the smoke
that rises from an opened peanut.
The couple is running out of things to say.

The couple is running out of things to say.
The couple is hungry to make new friends:
drawing out acquaintances, giving dinner parties
with too much cheese,
forming mad crushes on another pair,
inviting them over for a pleasant evening
and discussing each of their statements after they leave.

The Imperialist stage of couples:
A four-legged beast
scouring the living rooms for new blood.
They must rediscover the teenage sweat
of getting past Saturday night.

Poem

We were lying in bed
where we often told the truth
your breasts for instance never lied
there was an honesty about the hardness
of my penis
or when it lay soft in its daydream

Afternoon is the best time to make love
and afterwards you can
take a long walk
to the Museum, noticing the clouds
reflected in black skyscraper glass
because you might as well notice something

Talk about the justice of the sky
how each sky that is dealt to us seems appropriate

the light in your green eyes catching mine
in our apartment facing the courtyard

On warm days when the air is too shallow
we turn the fan on
we move the chairs around
we go out as sunlight fades into the river
and I see myself in some future bachelorhood
trying to hold the leaves, a white bridge floating
over our tired bodies, our raw cheeks buzzing
from too much knowledge

I see me coming back to this neighborhood
alone, renting a room on the hill
to sit on the Sunday Times
and watch the baby strollers

the joggers, the quiet soda cans
floating up the river
and all my days given over to losing you

1949

If you were as alive as Veronica Lake
1949
in luminous tennis shorts beside the pool
    with hair bobbing over one eye

        you wouldn't need natural foods
        or a wilderness to noodle around

    backstage with forties dolls
    you'd breathe
    the air of Saddhus
    from their crushed kneecaps

and go see Duke Snider twirling his bat in Ebbets Field
    making the catches look easy
                sliding into
        Rita Hayworth with her home run thighs

    falling through the fingers of her long black glove

They gave it all away   it was easy
    giving and easy living

        the gladness of postwar cocaine
        and the crummy roadhouses with Ida Lupino

    pacing back and forth in a green trenchcoat
feeling just like Stendahl
                Nostalgic for the present
                      Billie

Holiday crooning:
        I'm so happy to be unhappy
        I'm so happy to be unhappy

You wouldn't need meditation to be alone
You were so isolated no living thing could
ever reach you
                    Wandering around 14th Street
                    with the amphibious crowds
to end up in a night club

                                    jawing away your vital essence
                    into the ears of second-string Lizabeth Scott

thinking where is Veronica? where's that enigmatic
intelligence   and then the spotlight   landed

      like a flying saucer over her lowcut velvet gown
and she smiled to the orchestra

            who for one moment were snapped out of their
      shoelace nod by her hush of glamour

and the murderers put away their gats
and the plot slithered away
                              like an embarrassed Buick
                              parked on a San Francisco
                              hill in reverse

and she opened her mouth
to sing

I can't remember what
after all I was only seven
and I wanted the violence to continue

Nose Job

When I was a child my mother saved every drawing,
every birthday card, every poem
I ever wrote and put them in a wicker trunk
along with the photo albums
and the tax returns, financial documents and leases.

The trunk was lost years ago
in one of the many dashes my family made
across Brooklyn, in orange U-haul trucks.
Now I don't speak much to my mother:
she's become a star.
I see her in the subways advertising Levy's Jewish Rye,
pretending to be Italian,
though she used to call them guineas.
The latest news is she's getting a nose job.
Imagine, at fifty-three years old!

Do you know what history it takes to build
a nose like my mother's?
how many Jewish kids got punched in the face
on the way home from Hebrew School
until they started developing a Lamarckian
proclivity for bulbous noses?

Before that surgeon comes down with his Cossack sabre
on my mother's nose
in fashionable Leroy Hospital,
I want to take him aside and tell him—
Listen, I have a huge oak desk
retired from the civil service,
with lots of storage space.
I know you have your job to do;
but save me the scraps.

The Ecstasy

You are not me, and I am never you
except for thirty seconds in a year
when ecstasy of coming,
laughing at the same time
or being cruel to know for certain
what the other's feeling
charge some recognition.

Not often when we talk though.
Undressing to the daily logs
of this petty boss, that compliment,
curling our lips at half-announced ambitions.

I tell you this during another night
of living next to you
without having said what was on our minds,
our bodies merely rubbing their fishy smells together.

The feelings keep piling up.
Will I ever find the time to tell you what is inside these trunks?

Maybe it's the fault of our language
but dreams are innocent and pictorial.
Then let our dreams speak for us
side by side, leg over leg,
an electroencephalographic kiss
flashing blue movies from temple
to temple, as we lie gagged in sleep.

Sleep on while I am talking
I am just arranging the curtains
over your naked breasts.
Love doesn't look too closely…

love looks very closely
the shock of beauty you gave me
the third rail that runs through our hospitality.
When will I follow you
over the fence to your tracks?

Split Ends

If I speak about the rim of dirt
around our lives,
the hair caught in the tub
the muffled motor joining our bodies
that kicks up, whirrs, resists, grinds to a halt

sparks, kicks up, whirrs, whirrs, resists

of the frayed rubber belt that our nerves become
from trying to explain to the other
to make the other fit

and if I speak about that tube of fat, that heehaw
mouthgum
of the beloved
bared at just the wrong moment
it's not to disgust you
(for I know you're beyond that)

but simply to alert you
simply to advise you

      that love is a matter between equals

and that it may be necessary to hear
a certain amount of repulsive family history
and that it may be necessary to watch a woman cry
redfaced and dribbling snot down her lips

and to hope never to be hurt like that
and to wish one could be

In the end it's always a comment
from childhood about one's physical appearance

that sticks
the way kids looked at her in fire drills
the suspicion that her mother dressed her funny
always another's hurt
that you can do nothing about
saving your energy
for that last Humpty-Dumpty job

                    smiling at the stranger on the escalator
                a little more distinguished, a bit more
            able to pull it off
          with that worldly melancholy that's
       not unattractive

but if you were for once not
to move from her clumsy fingers
taking the sorrow she leaks for your oil

if you were once to stay
to sink into that sorrow

then it would be necessary to confess
that you have also felt worthless, soiled
like damaged goods in an army surplus store
that even the hippies don't want

that you have also felt like
a rubber duck
good for nothing but quacking its mama's name
days and days at a stretch
mindless, abandoned in the tub
wanting to be taken care of
held and covered

The Eyes Don't Always Want to Stay Open

The eyes don't always want to stay open
Even the lake gets tired of looking
At morning sun
Flashing blindly between trees
Even God must get sick of looking
At U-turns and pizza crusted curbs
On the Upper West Side
Sick of the lovers with their clubfooted mistakes

Her eyes never closed
At night I felt them on my chest
Flinching like an incubated chick
That wants to be born but isn't

Even the angels must sicken from excitement
Titian himself would turn away from Venus
And walk out for a breath of air
Pretending to clean his brushes

Pity the fish that look on at the ocean's horrors
Hovering in seaweed—camouflaged
A poor kind of rest
Not until frogs do eyelids make their entrance
Not until recently did I realize you could
Walk out of a movie

I left her house at 9:30
Her street was lit with summer rain and thunder
The lamps sliced open like pink grapefruit
The bums on the museum steps saluting me
As I sang the song that goes 'Never Again'
Never again would I touch the rounded banister
Never again search the mailboxes for her name…

Madonna of the Masseuses

You are holding a candle as if
To put the flame in your mouth
You would like to drink something
Really hot because the air conditioning
Is on too strong, inside this purple pyramid
Where they have you giving Latin massages
11 till midnight on the second floor.

When they enter you hand them the guest book
And slap the blue faces
Of those who forget to breathe.

It's in the sauna that everyone relaxes.
The businessman puts on his lace panties
And his scalloped apricot nightgown
While in the corner the film critic
Collects his darkness, through the titles
That are neither film nor life.
And when no one is looking the knife sharpener
Fondles his pumice stone with eyes closed
And the street vendor kneels down
Before his white Sabrett wagon.

Even the family comes to unwind.
The father has his paper and marshmallow cookies
The mother weeping stuffs her mouth with veal
The son plays with his quiet compass
The daughter makes her origami moons.
Because of you we are all contented to sit
Perfectly beautiful in our confinements
Waiting for your understanding fingers
To touch us everywhere

Look at the Squirrel

"Look at the squirrel
dropping a nut on his foot."

You wanted not to talk about
you or me or us together again,
but to select a point out there.

Out there are paintings, stones,
funny-looking men
rolled away from us
like awnings, dreamy androgynous profiles
in trains, the day's delicatessen,
sweat.

I see what you mean.

Do you want to talk about it now?

To Your Boobs

when we break up
as break up we must
leave me your boobs
in a fur-lined box

tell your next lover
as I am a Marxist
all goods should flow
to him that loves them best

but if you won't let them
they'll creep out alone
and visit me at Christmastime

they'll ring my doorbell
looking shy as students
their pink eyes peeking
"we were just in the neighborhood—"

"Come in, Nadine and Josephine!
it gives my heart peace
to see such perfect bosoms
floating in space"

Fedora

Waiting with me for the crosstown bus
was a homely Jewish man
                                        about fifty-five
        in fedora mittens and overcoat
                and a young girl in a green prep uniform
with golden hair
the kind they used to call 'flaxen'
                I took no notice of her
                        busy as I was
        stealing the headlines off the man's newspaper
when suddenly I realized the man and the girl
                                        were together
        The man—her father?—waved goodbye
                        and stood faithfully on the curb
while I dangled next to her
                        busstrap
                                in my hooligan leather jacket
but he had eyes only for his daughter
                a fine girl!   a princess!
as classy as any Wasp
                And that came from my loins!

        The bus driver engaged the engine
        The daughter's eyes brightened and she waved
but he stood
                hugging the yellow line
                                like a stuffed owl

        She seemed embarrassed
        her goodbye grin had hung on for too long
        then I saw her substitute
        a more chiseled smile
                        the ridge of her cheekbone
                                        quivered

with a subtlety that chained him
      as tightly as it now unsprung their glance

             The bus pulled us away
    the schoolgirl's face turned dull
      her color shrank to pussy willow grey
      and I lost track of her
    among the fresher faces clamoring to be seen

Petit Mal

for David Shapiro

He will be lying in his double bed
Watching the ghost trains flare across the ceiling;
His forehead by the sweating water jug,
His toes in Asia

He is determined to stay up all night
For the illness they have waiting downstairs
In the pantry with the papered shelves,
With the old lady who cooks mushroom soup.

Who will they send up to keep him company?
Petit Mal, the red face who cheats
And cries when he loses? Bully Jaundice,
Pink Eye, Mumps and Measles, or *creepy* Poliomyelitis?

Maybe it's Dyslexia, the crazy rich girl with capped teeth—
Who needs her? Plus her stuckup friend Rubella.
If it must be a girl, just let it be Hemophilia
Or pretty, pretty Scarlet Fever!

He will be lying in his sunken mattress
The pajama bottom slipping off his waist
Listening to the voices and the hoarse catarrh
The diseases of the phonograph

Mother comes in smelling fresh and perfumed
With green tulle over her titanic breasts
I'm leaving now cookie, she bends over him
And he throws up on her dress

Now comes the time to love being alone
He wants the feeling never to stop
To celebrate the sobs that keep rushing in
Like messengers to the General's tent.

They're gone—some loose skin dangles from
His sweet dehydrated mouth
The rough blanket weeps against his arms
He feels the birth of his strength

Walking Backwards

to Dziga Vertov

If time went backwards the bread would
return to the bakeries,
and newspapers to the typewriter keys' chapped lips,
the paper to the tree, crying and holding tight,
the maple syrup shuffling its feet up the bark

Mothers would know their children again:
The rock star, returning with an embarrassed kiss at the door,
would unpack his bag and go into his old room
with the green lamp and homework blotter and ham radio
to stare at the ceiling, then see if he can pick up Tokyo

The walleyed security guard, hallucinating
in the bank, returns to the spot where
his eyeballs first began to pull apart,
like college friends after graduation

The pensive receptionist pretending to look busy,
in bed the night before with her jobless boyfriend;
the lovers moving from climax to foreplay
from wetness to uncertainty, looking for a sign

The parachutist faltering and stretching his neck
like a turtle, not knowing which way is up

People we thought we had done with
would hit us like boomerangs:
girls walked away from at mixers,
dentists with dirty jokes, gym teachers,
blacks in pale green uniforms
wiping the counter at Chock Full of Nuts.

Rush hour faces recorded for no reason
than the wish that it might draw them back for a second look
this one a bonus, this time for pleasure—

I am not saying it would be so simple
I am not even saying it would all be worthwhile
but something I do know: the beef would get its intestines back
and I would get you back
resting my hand one more time
on the horn of your waist

and we would see snow
returning to the empty clouds
like a guilty wife, covering her husband
in ferocious white kisses to make him forget

Solidarity with Mozambique

My bank teller offers me a cigarette
and says he's only working at this job
to buy a discotheque.
                In the giddy afternoon
when all else fizzes
        we share a cigarette
we feel cream-colored.

Childhood is over
We recognize each other easier now
like members of a scattered set
of dishes united in a thrift shop
             the nervous habits

digging in noses
fingers stuffed in mouths
to choke back the secret failure

No one can believe that after all
        this sifting through love's shrapnel
we are more than scars.
Old Russian women smile at me in passing
We bring ourselves to nod hello
        while the young wives folding
sheets in the laundromat
stare and stare ahead
at their shadows in the plateglass

      At last we learn to read the world
to walk it openly
           taking love
from the iron of a streetlamp
held in the kindness of those we will never see—
        the lighthouse that's brushing

its large unshaven fatherly cheek
                    against us
if only we could feel it!

Solidarity with the people lost in office jobs
Solidarity with the red hurt that glows
            from the center of women
Solidarity with the peaceful lines of moviegoers
Solidarity with all those who love the sunlight
            across a red formica table, who take
                their coffee in diners,
                who put away their morning newspaper

Solidarity with the clumsy organizers
Solidarity with the fathers in the park
Solidarity with the ringing in our heads
Solidarity with the bicyclists who wave
Solidarity with Mozambique

Satin Doll

Last Sunday George Soto fell off a roof in East Harlem
Georgie was my student   I don't get it
Some say you were into skag
                             and in Harlem
ODs have a way of being pushed off the roof

Some say you were flying on acid
         weird ghetto bird
But Enrique the wise argues
'when you're dead
they'll say anything about you
that you fucked your own grandmother'

The Georgie Soto I knew was naturally high
he woke up the class once to tell us
Julio Roldan was found hung in the Tombs
swearing the pigs did it
and the Young Lords have taken over a church

George designs a flag for the revolution
rifles across a field of
Julio Roldan's face

I take some of his classmates on a field trip
                 to Gonzalez Funeral Home

my supervisor worries
         'Make sure they stay the full forty minutes
         Don't let them cut out early.'
                 a ghoul…

As soon as I arrive I want to split
OK I've seen it

but the kids crowd around

The family of mourners
retreats before this bunch of rowdy niggers
& sinks into folding chairs
three little Spanish ladies
the size of mosquitoes   chatting
waiting for the music to begin

*

Georgie Soto
          propped up in his coffin
look like a faggot
          on all that white creamy satin
look like a Latin doll on a wedding cake

his plastic face keeps changing
                    in slow dissolves
first sweet-smiling Puerto Rican proud
then cheek sags onto chin like heavy icing
          the left side floats over to the right side
and he looks real sad now
                              heartsick

                                        moved

watching a great epic movie with tears in his eyes
freshets of sorrows flowing and roaring into the pit
of his casket from hospitals and mothers in housedresses

                              without husbands without money
beating their children in the sepia street lights

as columns of marching hoes right-face
down the hallway, going off and waking
to the aspirin taste of a disappointed suicide

and everyone grieving to the dead son George
who can do nothing about it…

he's starting to cry!

      his eyelashes tremble

            you're faking it man

      a white candy dove
      has no idea what's going on
      settling on a branch of orchids
      de Tia y Pelle

        beneath an ozone blue crucifix
        the clock saying he died at ten past ten

if Georgie won't speak up
   Georgie es pato   a faggot!

because only faggots would take that kind of treatment
laid out in a funky wooden box
and once they put you in there you can't get out

dead people are pathetic, man
dead people are   disgusting
they just want attention
dead people are copouts
and need to be set straight
need to be taught a lesson

   but mostly dead people are unreal
strips of linoleum curled in the sun
   jive antique waxworks with no sweat
no heart no blackheads no favorite groups no erections

no more untimely hardons for Georgie

Yo! Babying women on the corner
  no more Arab bellydances during coffee break
  no more hot fights with teachers
    or fist raised in OFF THE PIGS salute
      the motherly white orchids boast to everyone
        How gentle! How well-behaved!

Georgie all I see is your left side
I want to see the side that hit the ground
bruised and squashed like a battered eggplant
I close my eyes and see you in the box
your yellow cheeks and mustache and black suit
ripped on satin clouds
my guts are churning
you're trying to make me feel bad
but I won't fall for that
I'll look away
I keep looking
this shock is like perfume   the senses deaden
till pretty soon I've forgotten where I am
Skipper notices me scratching my face
                              that junkie's gesture
and covering my eyes
        (I wonder what they think about me now)

Florrie signs her name in the condolence book
next to her new friend Mary
and Nelson shakes his head:

                George don't look good. George
                look AWFUL
everybody's down on the mortician

        they shouldnta stuck so much powder on him
          when I took a breath the powder flew
                            right off his face
          they shoulda covered up that bruise more

    that bruise look nasty
  and did you see how weird they made his eyes look?

Sweet Pam walks over troubled, whispers
He ain't even got no bleeding heart
I'm stunned at her poetic understanding

but it turns out
bleeding heart
is just the term for
an expensive
red floral arrangement

    ●

Outside I take deep breaths
It's cold and the chestnut man starts a fire
on Lexington Avenue. The check-cashing
is crammed for Thanksgiving
A girl's maxi coat blows open
and the wind tickles
her great meaty leg

and the last thing I think about is you.

PART 2
THE DAILY ROUND

Indigestible

A friend called up saying he was in a pre-suicidal mood.
I told him to come over.
I'd pay for the taxi.
"Will you go back with me to my apartment if I start to panic?"
I told him I would.
He arrived feeling chipper.
He wanted some wine.
I gave him a little cold sauterne that had been sitting
around in the icebox three weeks.
He said it tasted sour.

He looked at all my photographs.
He said he was feeling better.
We went out to dinner,
But it had to be on Madison Avenue.
For some reason he trusted Madison Avenue whereas
    Lexington, Third, Second and York were out to get him.
We sat in the last table far away from any draught.
I had my eyes on the delicatessen floor.
The radio was full of George Wallace being shot.
"Just like Huey Long," said my friend.
"Nixon did it
Now the gangsters are in the White House!"
I didn't argue.
My eyes were on my plate, Stuffed Derma and french fries.
Indigestible.
Suddenly he asked: "Are you feeling closer to me...?"

Of course I was,
I loved him.
But I used different words so as not to frighten him.
His head vibrated like a top whirling so fast you can't see it
    spin.

We paid the check and I told him as we were walking along
     Fifth Avenue, to catch the park and its rusty sunset, that
     I was also going through a bad time.
I had pinned my hopes on a shallow woman.
Though I no longer wanted her I felt curiously enervated.
Why this pain in my abdomen.
"Very simple," explained my friend.
"You experience an expansion, joy, the energy flows into all
     parts of the body.
Then a contraction, blocked, everything goes to the stomach.
You're still in high energy.
But there's no release.
The result is despair."
"That's it exactly!" I said to him.
It was getting darker and the first fat raindrops spattered
     onto the canopies.
The doormen were slipping inside, I was too excited to care.
"Answer me one more thing: expansion, contraction,
     physiology, I understand perfectly.
But what is it that stops us, when we're so near to joy?"

Only now did I notice my friend had his mad look.
His eyes, always beautiful, slid into passing cars.
He begged me to stop talking but I wouldn't.
I challenged him to explain the connections.
This nightfall, the orange chocolate smell, the dumpy couple
     walking by.
"Look at them," he said. "They're not going crazy.
Because they're healthy?
Or because they can't feel enough, because they don't know
     how to feel it."

Just then I felt it!
Right through my body.
"I feel it! I know what you mean! I feel it too!"
I wanted him to know...

"I don't think I'll wait for a bus," he said and jumped into a cab. His face wobbled against the wet glass.

The next day he was still alive.
Still alive.

Numbness

I have not felt a thing for weeks.
But getting up and going to work on time
I did what needed to be done, then rushed home.
And even the main streets, those ancient charmers,
Failed to amuse me, and the fight between
The upstairs couple was nothing but loud noise.
None of it touched me, except as an irritation,
And though I knew I could stop
And enjoy if I wanted to
The karate excitement and the crowd
That often gathers in front of funeral homes,
I denied myself these dependable pleasures,
The tricks of anti-depression
That had taken me so long to learn,
By now worn smooth with use, like bowling alleys in my soul.
And certain records that one can't hear without
Breaking into a smile, I refused to listen to
In order to find out what it would be like
To be cleansed of enthusiasm,
And to learn to honor my emptiness,
My indifference, myself at zero degrees.

More than any desire to indulge the numbness
I wanted to be free of the bullying urge to feel,
Or to care, or to sympathize.
I have always dreaded admitting I was unfeeling
From the time my father called me 'a cold fish,'
And I thought he might be right, at nine years old
And ever since I have run around convincing everyone
What a passionate, sympathetic person I am.

I would have said no poetry can come
From a lack of enthusiasm; yet how much of my life,
Of anyone's life, is spent in neutral gear?

The economics of emotions demand it.
Those rare intensities of love and anguish
Are cheapened when you swamp them with souped-up ebulliences,
A professional liveliness that wears so thin.
There must be a poetry for that other state
When I am feeling precisely nothing, there must
Be an interesting way to write about it.
There are continents of numbness to discover
If I could have the patience or the courage.

But supposing numbness were only a disguised disappointment?
A veil for anger? Then it would have no right to attention
In and of itself, and one would always have to push on,
Push on, to the real source of the trouble—
Which means, back to melodrama.
Is the neutral state a cover for unhappiness,
Or do I make myself impatient and unhappy
To avoid my basic nature, which is passive and low-key?
And if I knew the answer,
Would it make any difference in my life?
At bottom I feel something stubborn as ice fields,
Like sorrow or endurance, propelling me.

The Dowagers of New York

1.

The dowagers of New York in Persian lamb
with orange scarves around stringmeat necks
turn up at every movie matinee,
then fall asleep in their seats.
"I wasted ten dollars on this tripe."
At the ballet, the opera,
"I doze. It's nothing.
I like to listen with my eyes closed."

2.

New York is an Eastern European city,
a kingdom for dowagers' faces.
Old lady, you have the profile
of a mighty statesman, Disraeli.
But what happened to the rest of your body?
The middle went away.
And now you look so clutchy in the crosstown bus,
trying to win approval from the old woman next to you
with swollen legs who nods, shakes her head,
without really listening to a word.

"I have an extra ticket to the Noel Coward play;
it's supposed to be very well done.
This is where I get off. March 28th on a Saturday,
can you come? Don't forget!
Mark it in your calendar book!"

                                                    She's on the sidewalk

Now where? Some coffee,
a little lunch, a napoleon.

She takes her sweet tooth very seriously.
So wealthy and so foolish, how does she manage
to get through the weeks, waiting while
her husband rounds out his last years of practice?

Her wiser sisters have all flown South,
leaving her, like a retarded starling
in this cold museum city, the Moscow of America
to peck at a few crumbs
of pastry and culture.

Film Noir

for Tom Luddy

A large-shouldered man with short hair fingers his hat
While a beautiful woman paces impatiently in her morning-robe
With a cigarette burning beneath lipstick mouth.
"What's this about your husband, Miss?"
"That isn't why I called you here." She fixes him a drink.
The man lets his creased hat drop on the coffee table.
He can take in the house at a glance.
There are lamps on end-tables, mail-order furniture,
Glass animals and liquor, but no books,
And everything has been pushed into corners.
The place is too dark. Venetian blinds speckled with soot.
And the curtains are never quite open.
A two-step from the living-room is the bedroom.
Ah, lonely American decor of working-class houses near train tracks,
Where the men go off for days on railroad runs
And the wives pace in lowcut negligees, smoking
And plotting murder.

She wasn't evil, she wasn't a killer, she was just
Born poor and didn't know any better
So she grabbed the first man she could
After her boss got tired of her.
She grabbed a big hunk of man, ugly but honest;
He made an honest living, drove a big brute locomotive
But how could she have known that big-shouldered
Didn't mean good in bed. In fact he was a disaster.
Then the man in the hat came along.
He also had big shoulders, but he was good in bed.

They thought of running away together

But without money they wouldn't get far.
And poverty was no lark, she knew that; soon they'd
Turn on each other and life would be wretched.
So she figured out a plan. At first he didn't want to
Go along with it, because her husband was an all-right guy
But soon she persuaded him with her passionate figure
Which she paraded before him day and night in corset stays,
And her lipstick mouth sapped him, he knew lust;
And he got tired of meeting in hotel rooms to make love,
And besides, he was a weak character, though he could
Lift a sink, but from a moral point of view, he was weak.

Well, that's the story. They both got the electric chair.
In one version she gets accidentally strangled by a telephone cord.
In another he disappears and hits Skid Row unshaven.
But always there's that haunting smoke, between railroad cars
Where they go to ditch the body,

And always there's that flesh-love that no one can take away.

The Bum

Recently I saw a raggedy bum
take out his dick in the subway
and prepare to piss against the tile wall

Then he saw me and shrugged
as if to say, What can I do, I'm a failure I can't hold it in

I should figure out a way to write this as a haiku

Canto LXXXIX

"How much are you paying for your place?"

"Too much. 1800."

"That's not bad for a studio. I've seen worse."

"I've seen worse also. I've looked at studios for 2300."

"It's crazy."

"Sure it's crazy. For one little room and a kitchenette? You could rent a whole house for that."

"You're paying for the convenience of living in midtown."

"I think I'd rather live in the country."

"You said you didn't want to be in the country."

"I'm not so sure about this setup anymore."

"You think you'll try the country eventually?"

"Who knows?"

"A friend of mine got a one-bedroom apartment with a backyard and fixed it up beautiful."

"How much was she paying?"

"I think it was $3250."

"Well, sure."

"It really looked beautiful. That's the only way you can get a nice place."

"On my salary the rent I'm paying now is already too much for me."

"I thought teachers made good money."

"I make just enough. If he raises the rent on me I'll be in trouble."

"How much can he raise it by?"

"Seven per cent?"

"I think the maximum is fifteen per cent."

"Fifteen per cent is a lot. On 1800 that's what—$300?"

"No. Ten per cent is $180. Fifteen per cent would be 180 plus 90. $2700. Still, that's a lot to pay for your studio: twenty-seven hundred dollars."

"I'll have to move out."

"Lofts are expensive too. Just in the last few years the prices of lofts have skyrocketed. Everybody's looking for a loft."

"Everybody's looking, period."

"It's true, that's the problem. Everybody's looking. And then they want key money."

"I won't give any key money."

"Sometimes you have to. A friend of mine got a fantastic four-room place for $860 a month. But she had to slip the janitor $10, 000."

"It's unfair, $860 a month."

"I don't even like to go over and visit. I sit on the couch eating my heart out."

"That's what gets me so furious. You pay lavish rents and you get nothing in return. Nothing. Nothing! I would sooner buy into a townhouse with other people."

"That's not a bad idea, a townhouse."

"I don't know if a townhouse is such a great idea either."

"And townhouses can be very expensive too."

15

It's Painful Getting Letters

It's painful getting letters from those
you love only a little, and who
think you're their best friend.
They write you four page laments and you
return one, three months later
full of hasty regrets.
You would like to love them completely
for what they are, as their mother loved them
(or didn't love them), but as you watch them flounder
in blandness and self-pity from one world capital to the next,
you can't escape the thought that they can do nothing for you,
unless it be to teach you a little more about
the sinking strategies of survival.
Each letter ends with a more passionately imagined rendezvous
which begins to sound like a threat:
"Have so much to tell in person—
I hope to come up through New Hampshire this July."
"Maybe we'll visit Denmark after all!"
So by now you can see inside out the day when
you two *will* be together, facing the stream
and pretending that beautiful Nature has made you silent.

Indian Winter

Inferior to the day,
Which is beautiful and mild,
Unseasonably gentle,
I cross the park
Observing nothing,
Alone in my mind,
On a Saturday afternoon,
With everyone strolling
To catch the sun
And almost against
My will I notice
A young man with a baby
Riding on his back,
Two old ladies in my way,
And I am thinking: "Come on, you must. Of course live."
That was no noble decision,
No more than a marble
Dropped onto the sidewalk
Continues to roll.

Not Sadness Which Is Always There

After I had learned to live with my sadness
There came another, more disturbing strangeness
Whose purpose I could never understand, who always came late at night

And who kept me awake all hours
Until I turned on the headlamp to read,
As if finally forced to concede,

Not understanding that some things have nothing to do with the Will.
I who had conducted my life so that
I could not do other than what I do,

Who had steered my heavy ship around and around
Until it could only steer in one direction,
I saw no way to put this turmoil to good use.

It was not sadness, which is always there
like a cat I raised from childhood and stroke absent-mindedly
While going on with my work;

Not even loneliness, which I had trained to back down
In the presence of good company,
But something more needy.

Even as I sit with friends in the Hungarian pastry shop
Dawdling over sweets,
I am shaken by the urge to run home

To be alone with it, to let it work me over,
The mice combing the bag of day-old crumbs
Raking my stomach for overlooked mistakes.

Yellow Bird

The day after Thanksgiving I went into the Drago Shoe Shine Parlor to get my once a year shine. The streets were churning with bloated strollers on holiday, their bodies dulled by half-digested turkey, and faces with thoughtful frowns attentive to the lower regions. Slowed down overnight, they had evolved into a race of philosophers. The owner of the shoe store stood in the doorway looking for something bright to catch his eye.

I took possession of my throne without much fuss. The red stuffed vinyl gave out a hiss when I sat down. I would have loved to prolong this imperial moment by reaching to my left for a magazine, but unfortunately I was the only customer. A black in a short-sleeved green uniform began to apply himself to my feet, without any personal bitterness, but philosophically, sudsing the corners with a peachy mush.

Leaning against the display counter was a young Jamaican I had not noticed before. He was brownskinned, and dressed in a very sporty outfit—jockey cap, lemon jacket, tight-fitting lemon pants. It was not so much that the costume was dramatic as that it seemed so coordinated, so up-to-date, so cunning and yet unimpeachably correct. Almost, I found myself thinking, like a pimp's outfit.

Suddenly he began to sing.

> *Yellow bird, why do you fly away?*
> *Yellow bird, why do you fly away?*
> *Did your little wife*
> *Leave your little nest?*
> *Did she fly away*
> *Leaving you to stay?*

He sang the song right through, crooning it with impeccable suaveness like Nat King Cole, and the breezes that blow through an island beach. No one gave the slightest indication of hearing him, least of all the burly man brushing my shoes. The singer's own eyes were sullen, opaque, refusing to give in to the lyrics of the song. The song flew out of him against his will; its moment had come to escape. If he were being handcuffed at that moment he would sing it, if he were being led away, if he were standing beside the grave of his mother he would have to sing the silly song about the yellow bird.

Da da da da da... what does he care about the yellow bird? What did the bird ever do for him? It is possible that he beats women across the face, it is quite possible that they would give anything to see him once in this tender mood which breaks out only in the rarest moments of self-forgetfulness, leaning against a shoe counter, waiting for a business appointment.

And when he finished the last note, he walked straight out of the store.

Allende

In 200 years they won't remember me, Salvador
And they won't remember you, so let's skip the part about
He will live with us forever.
You may get a footnote for being the only Marxist
To gain power in Latin America via parliamentary means;
And the only sucker not to throw his enemies in jail.
You knew the power of the large land-owners, ITT,
The Army, U.S. Anaconda, the small frightened businessmen
Easily manipulated, the shop-owners who could go either way
And yet you didn't lift a finger to silence them.
You continued to defend the bicameral system of government
Until they bombed your palace and you shot yourself in the mouth.
Answer me this,
Now that you are a bunch of hairs on a blood-stained sofa:
I want to know why you killed yourself.
Because this was a very un-Marxist thing to do.
Because neither was this the way of a gradualist
With short graying hair and glasses,
    and a face like a prominent surgeon's,
Who, knowing this would happen, could have easily arranged for
The secret tunnel, the private plane, the unmarked car
In which you, huddled in grandmotherly wig, might begin
To write your memoirs. Was it too horrible to think of
Speaking at New York rallies to pockets of émigrés,
Forming shadow cabinets, and lunching with Juan Bosch
Or Andreas Papandreou, swapping stories over wine about
Where you were when the shit hit the fan?
I'm being vulgar, forgive me.
I would rather believe in your doggish retreat
Than the flamboyance of today's headlines which gloat:
MARXIST REPORTED TO TAKE HIS LIFE.
Even they are a little unsure. They leave room
    for the graduate students
Of the left, working in the carrels of libraries

For 100 years to discover the link,
The way it all fits together: Lumumba, King, Kennedy,
    Allende, CIA.

And it may turn out that my government actually murdered you
But what's the good of knowing that?
We know too many connections already, and they only satisfy
The pedantic urge that makes the world a crossword puzzle.
Salvador, I'm sorry, I don't know what to say any more.
Take back the bullet, it was a mistake, it redeems nothing.

Today I look at the faces of passers-by and I think:
It figures. The banks have the money to buy counter-revolution,
This wino has no money. He's nice enough, so is
That girl in the flamingo summer dress on wobbly heels.
It's September 12, possibly the prettiest day of the year.
The blue has never been so pure around the chimneys—
"Almost like—a cartoon!" says the dental hygienist,
Grasping for a metaphor. I never said it even to myself,
Before today, but just between you and me,
And I don't want anyone else to hear: Senor.
It looks as if they have got us by the balls.
These faces in the street, how can they take power?
How can they rule?

Blue Pants

If you follow your feet
                    you end up in the marketplace
                    because that's all you want
                    is the crush of slobs
                    drooling black sausage
                                        grease
            on table after oilcloth covered table

Orchard Street Petticoat Lane the Plaka la Marqueta
                    les Marches aux Puces
                with the gypsy scarves   old suits
                    78 gramophone records
Empty Saturday processions through church bazaars
                looking for a silver saltshaker
                    or a shoelace
                            but it had to be the right shoelace

In Amsterdam once the sorethroat Dutch rain
                caught up with me in an open market
                    soaked the shishkebabs
                            sizzled the fires
                tarps tented down over stands

A badtempered afternoon   with nothing to say for it
            I had time to kill
                            before night
when the women took up their doorways under red light
                    bulbs along the canal
                        The water is black
                    and it came as a shock
                            to find my pocket picked
                though later on it all made sense

What did I expect?

Anyway, marketplaces:
I started going when I was a boy
My mother took me to the city market
          where Havemeyer Street ended, in Brooklyn

Ladies lowering their shopping carts
          inch by inch
                    over the curb
          careful with the eggs on top

Some little coughing girl was always getting it
          "COVER YOUR MOUTH!" I felt glad
                    it wasn't me

          Childhood is standing by the curb
waiting for a lady to finish
talking to another lady
in a flower print dress
wondering if it's safe
to cross the street
          Sometimes you get a smack

          But I hold on because   it's worse
                    to lose my mother's hand
          and run up and down
                    vegetable stalls
with a few tears and the briny smell of
          sour pickles making me hungry
And "Damn! Damn! where'd my mother go?"
                    cursing bad luck
          while trying to look grownup and curious
                    for the others

It all comes back later in a funny dream
          the one where I'm walking along the thoroughfare
                    with my heart's delight   and the camera moves
          a little to the right

                          a closeup of my smile
          so that I don't even notice love
                  passing out of the frame
                  like the railing of a streetcar
          until I realize her hand is gone
          and there's nothing else to notice
                          or to mourn

But I wanted to tell you the story about the blue pants.
I'm determined to get that story out of the way
          Do you suppose a new life
                          could start for a man
                          if he told an anecdote perfectly?
A story, let's say
          that clouds his thoughts for years
                          until one day he shouts
          Enough! Get away from me!
          I don't care any more about the blue pants!
                  You could strangle me   I'm not
                          telling it again
                  I'll write it down once, then leave me alone.

My mother had taken me to the marketplace
          to buy a new pair of pants.
Try to imagine what embarrassment for an eight year old boy
          to have his mother apprise his figure
                                  an entire afternoon
Nothing could be worse, you'd think.
I was looking forward to it.
                  The gypsy ladies in windbreakers
                          tried to catch her eye
                  with velvet swatches   calico
                                          housedresses
                  "Something for the young man?
                          Earmuffs?"
but this time she skipped all the street bargains
and took me into a decent store.

                    The man had a measuring tape
around his shoulders
                    Bushy mustache bushy eyebrows
                              sunken eye sockets
            and only half an inch taller than I.
How could it be otherwise with the shop
        so narrow that only a runt could pass between
            the suitracks and the shelves
                    jutting with boxes
                              half shoved-in shoved-out

        "What color is he looking for?"
"Something in black or charcoal grey," I heard
        my mother say.
                "Step this way."

Then I saw a pair of blue cotton pants
        the most beautiful pants in my life
                    A royal blue
        that sopped up all the joy in the ocean
                and mocked the sooty dark Brooklyn clouds

                              How could you be sad
            knowing you had a pair of such wild pants
                to put on next morning
                        and make the rounds with?

        like the blue porthole that hypnotizes you
        like the blue shark,
        that kind of blue

"Don't you think?" said
                my mother, "they're a little too loud?"
I knew right away
that whatever she was trying to tell me
was no good for the blue pants.

But what was her objection?
The salesman and she seemed to share the joke
"Take it from me cookie you don't want these pants.
They look awfully good to you now
but in a week
you'll be tired of them. They're—*garish*,
you understand?"
Garish? Loud?
I understood that she had the money.
Without a struggle   too proud
I let them slip from my hands.
Let me turn my face from their blinding blue ray
let me examine these charcoal greys
these browns my mother said
go good with my eyes.
Maybe even this old man pinstripe
has something to say for it.

Sad business herringbone   O lugubrious worsteds
though I took several from the pile of
distinguished weaves,
they were heavy and I wanted to
float light and cottony above the world!

In the cardboard dressing room
with three brass hooks
I let my khaki chinos shiver to the floor
Poor chinos I had also loved you once
thought you'd open every door for me
Now you were used up and I
sweating in baggy wool
before two mirrors that caught my profile
at an angle I never wanted to see again
the crooked nose, the cowlick
the earnest earnest Austrian cadet's eyes—
listening to my mother
behind the partition flirt with the salesman

talking about children's wear and the high cost of meat
      I surprised her.

"Those aren't bad. Turn around...
They're a little baggy around the seat."
I went back
and tried on the brown with droopy pleats.
I was curious how much ugliness
she would make me swallow.
                  "I like that color on you" she said
                    "How do they fit?"
            They fit okay, I shrugged.
                  (I wasn't giving much.)

She whispered me into a nest of suits.
     "Listen, I know you still feel bad
    about the blue pants. Right?"
         "No I forgot about them."
    "The reason I wouldn't let you have them
        is that those are the pants,"
                she lowered her voice,
        "all the Puerto Ricans wear.
    They're gaudy! not in good taste
        You don't want to go around
    looking like a Puerto Rican do you?"

"No." I looked at her level and innocent
till shame had filled her chubby face,
like cherry Kool Aid in a pitcher.
She was not a bigoted woman, she tried to be enlightened,
she did the best she could in raising us.
I stick to this banner
though all the schools of psychotherapy leer
though Panzer tanks of women shrinks
roll over her fallen shield in their efforts
to embrace me, I stick to this

to my last dying breath: For all her faults
My mother was essentially *not a bad woman.*

        I wanted that shameful look in her eyes to go away
           I wished I could find a new pair of pants
               and fall in love with them, earnestly
                  so that my mother would feel all right.
        But I couldn't.
            My face was sulking.
            There was nothing I could do about my face!

            "Look,
      you still want those crazy blue ones?
          Try them on."

      I snatched them into the dressing room
          before she could change her mind.
Now comes the part I don't know how to tell.
        Maybe I had waited too long.
Like a beautiful underwater rock
       the diver brings up to the surface
          only to watch its vibrant colors fade
             in the air, that brilliant blue
                died a little when I put it on.
        I suddenly understood
        how common they were.

Love
      had played its first trick on me
I was frightened by my own fickleness
How could I know that the radiance comes and goes?
      I didn't have the heart to admit
that I no longer cared for them
         There was no turning back now
            I put on a brave smile of gratitude
        and issued forth   ready
          to convince her that she had made me

the happiest boy

My mother was in terrific spirits
She came home and told everyone
how she had indulged my cockeyed tastes
The neighbors said,
he has to learn
by his own mistakes
They had a good laugh

I stored the pants on a hanger
way back in the closet
where I could barely reach them
Once or twice I wore my blue pants to school
I wished them an evil fate

and was glad
when I found them
kicked and tarstained on the closet floor

So much for getting what you want, I thought
and closed the door on happiness
for many years

Maybe that's an exaggeration
Anyway you've heard the story
Some story, eh?

Probably I didn't tell it right
I still don't know whether to feel charmed or angry!

Scars end up as decorations
it doesn't matter—
In this life, who knows
who will have the final word,
the hurt or the blue?

Rumors

The whole fifth grade was
suddenly amok with love
Someone had thrown Jonas
against Teresa
in a game of catch-the-girls
And Jonas said I'm sorry
She'd felt her arm slide over his
Next Saturday he took her
to the movies—or so she says
and bought her a bracelet
with two hearts, and
a stuffed felt lion.

Meanwhile David had thrown over
serious-minded Tanya
and showed interest in Wanda,
his former enemy—
after telling everyone
he couldn't stand her guts.
And Wanda knew David's telephone number
by heart.
She told it to her cousin
who called David and said:
What do you think of Wanda?
And David screamed:
I can't stand her guts!
But Wanda knew he'd asked her out
and had to keep their secret
from the world,
and that was just his way.

The others who were not involved
in this romantic life—
the slow ones, the workers,

the short boys—
hated the lovers and called them
brown-noses.
They thought that love meant
sticking one's nose
up a girl's behind.
But Christine, the tall mild grownup
girl who wrote about horses,
thought everyone was acting very childish,
and wondered if the teacher
needed help straightening off
her desk, which looked a mess,
or marking present-and-absent
in the rollbook.

Charlotte Russe

Charlotte Russe, whipped cream with a dab of shortcake
      inside a cardboard hatbox
                  which
         turned over
              reveals a false bottom
     Half cake half air
        dissolving in the mouth on contact
no matter how you try to prolong it

         A cheat   this Charlotte
       like Marlene in *The Scarlet*
Empress whose crinolines and
                rouge
beguile horsemen down staircases
      to the
         grotto bedroom
where they clutch
        a phantom flesh
all gauze and veils   a trick
      like the obliging women who open
  their dresses to you in dreams

Old whipped cream swindle
      But what's more fun
   than to be taken with your eyes open

It was in my senior year
      I had passed my Algebra regents.
        I left the muddy doors
   of the high school entrance
crowded with grubs comparing answers—as if
         that could help them now
     and thinking I deserved a special gift
       for getting such a high mark

          on a test which, after all,
                  "wasn't even my subject"
      I bought myself for fifteen cents
        a Charlotte Russe

That year I piled triumph upon triumph.
Exam after exam fell
before my magnetized pencil.
Valedictorian
Most Likely to Succeed
The Chamber of Commerce Award—
who could I take along my lonely walks
to share the raptures
of enumeration?
Self-astonished at every moment
I had no one to tell but
the elevated trains, roaring over me
like Gods with stomach pains

Where was my *equal*,
         where was there someone to join in my rejoicing,
      what was I supposed to do with this miraculous
                      energy?
I was so powerful I could shake the girders if I dared!

In the end it was painful.
You have to return to a
normal life.
I bought a Charlotte Russe at the bakery
under the El:

          A rush of sweetness
            then dissolution,
   disenchantment, the slow ironic smile relaxing
          to a more comatose well-being
Came graduation—
What speeches I gave!

when it ended I was more alone than ever
People clap to feel their palms smack together
Friends smiled but I kept looking for
the black dot in their eyeballs.
The parents you could forget about—
They knew too well how to spike
any compliment with their own lament

Only you, Charlotte
                        understood me
            You realized I wanted nothing more
                    than a little sweetness
            a kiss of gentle confection
                    to ease me down to human scale,
                            where I could disappear
                                            among the rest

            Not constancy   no special favors
                only that when I came to you   tired
                you would be fresh and worldly-wise

    and let me bury my nose in your white ermine muff!

Once A Long Time Ago

Once a long time ago, you remember
we were living in the basement of our parent's house
we two brothers, the girls sharing a room upstairs
It was dark in the basement, dark and hard to move around
and our sister charged her friends a dime
to visit, calling it the Spook House.
      I would look up from my book
sometimes and see a line of ten year olds in pink shorts
climbing down the trap door steps.
What are you doing here? I asked calmly
never realizing I was the spookiest part of all
The little girls giggled and ran for help
Maybe you don't remember that
You were too busy looking for a job

      Maybe you remember how we slept together
next to the oil burner
on an old double mattress, getting along,
two friends, never complaining about privacy
until one afternoon around four-thirty
I came across you, my older brother, older
and ashamed to be living under his mother's roof,
your legs hanging out of a green, sour-smelling topsheet,
your black hair mussed, your stallion's eyes desperate
like horses trapped in a flaming barn.
You wouldn't look at me.
               I asked you what was wrong
you remember? But instead of answering your whole body
    shrunk
and when I got into bed beside you
you started to cry   you started to cry but no sound came out
and I was wondering if you were faking
or if there was so much that wanted to come out

that you had to hold a pillow over it
		and smother it

I never told you this but Esquire Magazine was lying
on the floor face up, the new issue, and I wondered
if something you had seen there had made you unhappy
like the disgusting Bourbon ads, or the dense novelettes
that left me slightly nauseous like cups of warm water

I also wished I could look at the new issue
I had time for many thoughts because you took a while crying
and I couldn't think of anything to do except hold you
and keep asking what was wrong
I felt confident in the end you would tell me
and this is perhaps what you could never forgive me
My conqueror's belief in the absolute power of sympathy
because you never did tell me
and I saw that you didn't trust me enough
and I still don't know to this day
what was wrong
because all you said was

"Leave me alone, just leave me alone for two minutes."

The People on the First Floor

There must be a house where sunlight
falls on and on on the bedspread;
maybe a cherry tree outside,
and in the window ledge a kleenex box
with one lilac tissue collecting dust.
I keep looking into people's apartments on the first floor.
Red-flowered geraniums are common
and upholstered chairs with gold fringes and
families walking around in their undershirts.

It breaks my heart, those comfortable first floor interiors.
How they set up a reading corner with one cool blue lamp
against the heckling street,
the plump foot hassock resting there...
But even mildewed Slavic tenements have their grace notes:
a calendar, a boy's toy car,
a meaty arm filling the windowsill.

Who are these citizens who consent to live
in full view, offering their placid ordinariness
to a city desperate for lucid models?
Maybe saints. Maybe cranks. Manikins?
They sit in the dark
and their furnishings overwhelm them
like the homey darkness that grows around a blind man.

Furnished Room

When you live in a furnished room
the world starts to resemble a furnished room.
Even when you go out on the street,
people with winter coats on look like furnished rooms.

Your room is never heated properly,
you are always chilly and hoping
to warm up in restaurants.
You buy a coffee, you make the pretense
of loving your paperback book,
an hour to waste before the show,
you grab at the immaculate bathroom
of a college student center
where you read a leaflet on the floor which means
absolutely nothing to you,
as if you were forced to repeat a course
in Spanish,
or take a long pleasure holiday in a rainy place.

Later you mingle near a crowd of strangers
at intermission.
Your skin is flushed and you listen to their conversation
and you are almost ecstatic and you
have to return to your furnished room
with the tall ceilings
which are unusual for their antique molding
but why does one need such a high ceiling?
Better to live under the bed than to have that high ceiling!

The night will find you, and the covered quilt
and the newscaster's voice
will seep in like an odorless gas,
and the upstairs boarder's shoes
 will grind down on your chest,

and is it true that you are lost
in this one furnished room
with no home but this
And am I really lost, for good,
under the furnished stars

Saturday on the West Side of Assisi

Saturday morning put on a record make coffee
and dance in front of the mirror
You're not Fred Astaire but you'll do
as you whisper "I love I love I lo-ove her!"
but whom do you love, remember?
Saturday. Only Saturday.
The coffee smells good and you know exactly when to turn it off.
Sip it on a stuffed chair looking at the thin light
spoon itself, like sugar, onto the dusty rose carpet
Those special pink dyes only the Chinese know—
This isn't one of them.
Can't get rugs like that out of Peking any more.

Later you water the plants and walk to the lake
Watch the long-distance runners with numbered orange
         tee shirts
and the slow lazy couples who have just got up from sex,
cruising the windows of antique shops for a lamp.
You come back home and read a long numbing article
in The New York Review of Books on Conrad
By that time it will be three o'clock and you've
run out of momentum. Time to make new decisions
get on the phone: Who wants to go to the movies tonight?

This is my life. I have no complaints.
If I were a family man I could spend weekends responding
to my children's cuts and yells,
never have to think too far in advance. Maybe lock myself
in the rec room for hours reading every word of Proust.
No, I'd be happy.
Grant that much to the future.
The birds
would hop above my deckchair in what suburban sunset?

But the birds sing even on West 71st Street,
and I am Saint Francis of Assisi.

It's Good We Only See Each Other Once a Week

It's good we only see each other once a week.
A young man about to move in with his fiancée
died of a sudden heart attack at twenty-six.
One hears these stories all the time.
The heart is trained to handle deprivation,
not unforeseen happiness. Just as when you
throw your arms around me I start to overflow,
but then I think of course, where was she before?
I deserve it and a lot more besides—
your love gets soaked up quickly
and I pull back brooding over something
I never had.
But don't stop on that account, keep going.

I was brought up to make
the most of accidental brushes with kindness.
My pleasures were collected almost unawares
from stationary models, like the girl
who sat in front of me in tenth grade,
who let me stroke and braid her golden hair
and never acknowledged it.
I wouldn't know what to do with frontal love;
would I? One snowy winter night in Montreal
I felt so great I danced a flamenco
and insisted that everyone call me Fernando.
But then I was by myself. And last night,
if there are many more nights
like last night with you—
when I think of all my nights of total happiness
I get the panicky sense that the balance
has already tipped,

and I will never again feel free
to pass myself off as a have-not.

Maybe it's good we only see each other once a week.
But don't stop on that account, keep going.

The Thrill of the First Night

I love the first night when I sleep with someone new
And even more I love the second night
But the third night can be problematical
The fourth night is enjoyable
In a quiet way
Though often it doesn't get to a fourth night

And after all the love has run its course
I love to walk around the girders
In a city park
Maybe holding up a viaduct or highway exit
And think that all this green, like so much cabbage
Or stinkweed on a humid day,
And the broken glass and fieldstone walls and steps
To walk down quickly looking over your shoulder,
Will still be around when they throw you over.

Ode to Senility

The ultraviolet night-light in the florist's
seen from a bedroom window, 6:15
Hour of furry dawn, no one is up yet
I leave the woman's house before her daughter wakes up
I wish I could tell this girl I mean her mother no harm
The woman goes back to sleep, I close the latch behind me
I am old, old, old
I start to fall asleep in the taxi
I climb the brownstone steps with a full bladder
With one gesture I fling off my coat and open the door
I am tired and I curl up on my bed
I am realizing my lifelong ambition, to grow old

I want to be eighty and have people whisper about me
in gatherings: He was a Communist,
he was the first to take acid
the earliest to recognize the System was rotten
And look how serenely he carries himself
such vibrant eyes   how well-preserved
these men of conviction remain!

Let them think I had a crazy youth
that blondes in furs beat down my door

I want to be eighty and tell anecdotes
the same five anecdotes
about the time I outwitted the tax service

I want to be old and tiresome and able
to forget those caresses
turning self-reflective on the thigh
forget the daughter in the next room

I know enough about the light behind the shadow behind the light
behind the marble on the terrace in the morning
and on everyone's faces

let me grow senile enough to watch
with gumless charity the pretty woman
squirming on a man's lap in the empty bus—
thinking,
Who are all these children who call me grandfather?
I don't remember marrying.
Which one of them did I finally love now,
Which one of them decided to put up with me?

The Woman Who Cried for Nothing

He introduced her to some friends in the street:
"This is a woman who cries for nothing."
Because after she flew to Sao Paolo to visit him
And the first day he was happy to see her;
And the second day he was pressed with life-worries;
And on the third day he was sad about
      taking a friend to the hospital
And the fourth day he threw his arms around her
      before everyone at the party and said,
      "How can we not live together?"
And the fifth day he never called;
And on the sixth he listened deeply like an African to music;
 And the seventh he proposed
      that they go to a hotel and make love;
And on the eighth he would not help her buy a bus ticket;
And on the last day when she met him in the street,
He looked serene and vital and offered to carry her bags,
She burst into tears;
And he asked, "What are you crying for?"
And she said, "For nothing."

The Beautiful and the Ugly (A Play)

ACT 1.

Scene 1: A roomful of beautiful, stupid women making the most stupid conversation imaginable. One is telling fortunes from coffee grounds, another is complaining about a dirty spoon, and so on.

Scene 2: The couple in the restaurant. An ugly, brilliant man is talking to a ravishingly beautiful, stupid woman. The ugly, brilliant man is explaining about the Ottoman Empire.

Scene 3: A group of ugly, spiteful, brilliant women make sparkling conversation about the disappointments of love. They are a delight to listen to.

Scene 4: An ugly, brilliant woman and an ugly, brilliant man sitting in a restaurant. They analyze each other mercilessly.

ACT 2. The Half-Breed

Scene 1: A somewhat beautiful, somewhat homely, rather brilliant young woman is trying to fascinate an unbelievably good-looking rock 'n roll musician moron. In spite of the fact that the woman is wearing a scarlet satin blouse with the top four buttons unbuttoned, it is clear from certain gestures and dictions that she is a winner of a Woodrow Wilson Fellowship. The man asks her if she would like to smoke something, and she says "Sure."

Scene 2: The somewhat beautiful, somewhat homely, brilliant young woman is talking to her girl friend, another half-breed, and telling her the story of her date with the rock 'n roll moron. The friend listens silently with a knowing, judgmental half-smile. The story is that he has another girl-friend whom he lives with, but she managed to take him home with her. "He's extraordinarily sensitive in his own way. Uncanny—ability to know what I wanted. Not verbal—he's not very verbal, but an extraordinarily—odd use of language. I'm afraid I scared him." She giggles. Her friend keeps smiling.

Scene 3: A half-ugly, half-handsome, reasonably intelligent man flirts with a half-ugly, half-pretty, reasonably intelligent woman. They both confuse each other tremendously with double signals.

ACT 3.

Scene 1: A beautiful, brilliant, warm-hearted young woman appears. The playwright runs onto the stage and grabs her away, thus ending the play.

PERFORMANCE NOTE:

In the event it is impossible to find anyone suitable to play the part of the woman in Act 3, the play will be continued indefinitely, with the different characters combining and re-combining in any permutations that remain.

Penelope in Soho

You search his eyes for clues.
The loft bed that your husband built
So high it nailed you to the ceiling,
Before going off to spiritual India,
Now contains a second man.

"I want you to take me seriously.
Don't lie next to me and give me a taste of
The warm feelings I had learned to live without,
If you are only going to go away."

You search his eyes for clues.
But everyone is going to go away.
At the end of the loft is a round brass gong
That the sunlight ripples like a goldfish
And he stares at it, stares for all he's worth.

Sulky Sonnet

The cypresses hang in the brackish fog
Outside our room. You don't get up all day,
Skin smelling acrid from cigarettes.
Wanna orange? Your bloodshot eyes take in
My simpleminded offer with distrust.
What's wrong? You can't explain, it goes too deep.
Your urge to live is down to thirty watts.
The window string flaps like a cripple's hand.
I'd love to ride a bike along the marina
All by myself, when sunset hits the water…
Then why do I stay cooped inside with you?
What holds me here? You don't want any chaperone
For this funk. You shut your eyes to doze
And I sit doting on your innocent toes.

The Time We Stayed in the Dead Artist's Shack

I wanted to lie in a casket beside you
And put my dead, reasonable flesh
Against your hysterical flesh, and row
Like two carved Vikings toward the stars

And I wanted you to love me for it.
You hid in the tub, in this house
With cows painted on bathroom walls
And Paradise murals in the empty room.

The Queen of Paradise was depicted as a naked eight year old
(The artist's daughter Mary had sat for it).
The shack was full of the dead man's work.
Murky easel paintings I could just barely see

In the dark of late afternoon thunderstorms.
I felt helpless, nauseous, puny
Waiting for you to get out of the tub,
Not sure at all I trusted you.

You washed your hair and sat for a moment
On my bed with a yellow towel around you,
And I reached out
Like a spider crawling toward the moonlight.

The Court of the Two Sisters

The slow green fans turning in the courtyard
Of the classy restaurant in New Orleans;
The green napkins and the Negro waiters
Advancing in their bright green uniforms, superiorly
Filling the large water goblets dusty in the sun.
The hot rolls with curled butter shells like snails
And the enormous breakfasts served at all hours
Of Eggs with lemon sauce, asparagus, ham and toast points;
Cold creamed shrimp soup, oranges.
I read two newspapers at once, starting with sports;
Crowding the tablecloth with unwanted sections.
And when I was too stuffed to go on
I ordered a chickory coffee, dark and bitter
And a Charlotte Russe bursting with whipped cream.

The Deer Flies

They had taken me to a lone spooky spot,
An old beach where Indian pottery had been found,
Four thousand years old.
Sand crabs darted under dead timber.
The white sky glared whitely.
I stepped into the lukewarm Gulf Stream:
The tide was out, it was intolerably hot.
"You must find this oppressive," said Mary our hostess;
"The air is so close and still."

"Oh no," I said, "It's cool with my feet in the water."
Mary pointed out a rhinoceros beetle,
Then an armadillo hole. The flies were biting
At my legs and I had stupidly worn tennis shorts:
Baby blue shorts from Brooks Brothers!
Diane explained that the bugs were bad
When there was no wind. "It's a shame
There's no wind," said Mary. "It's usually
Not this buggy."

It started to rain. The rain bounced off
The calm ocean slanted, and wattled the sand
like chicken pocks or alligator skin.
I ran for the car but they dawdled, remarking
How much they loved a good storm.
I could love a good storm too, I supposed,
Holding myself back, soaking on the hill
While the sky opened and they dug their toes
In the sand below, two Mississippi girls
Remembering exciting storms, pointing at the cloud:
"That white glare around the edges
Means rain won't cool it off one bit."

We made it to the car. There were flies
In the back seat, all over the styrofoam picnic basket.
"Those deer flies! They're terrible today," Mary swore.
But she wanted to show us some woods near the beach
That was even more unspoiled,
So we wandered down the dirt path through the trees,
Flies and dragontails at my face.
"Won't the rain make them go away?" I whined.
—"Where they going to go? When they're out, they're out."
The backs of my knees were swollen,
My arms itched like demons, and I was waving
Both hands in front of me just to get by,

"Who owns this land?" I demanded.
— "The property belongs to a real estate man
From New Orleans. His wife is a bit of a Bohemian
And she loves the country out here."
— "I hope she loves the bugs as well,"
I said testily. At that my hostess
Stopped and thought a bit:
"No…I expect they stay in New Orleans
When the deer flies are out."

Someone in London

She had the whitest skin
and brown fingernail polish
and brown lipstick
and brownish red curly hair
and a dark brown satin skirt
and that marble-white skin
as if she were always about to faint
and she had a baby
and the baby had awfully white skin
and blonde hair
and the baby's father's name
was George
and he was somewhere in Brighton
trying to get back into school
And she was on Home relief
and she used to shoot heroin
and sometimes still did shoot heroin
when she ran into old bad friends
but then she felt guilty
for days, and nauseous.

She had once known a composer
of rock music when he was still
in art school, before he became big
whom she felt was the finest,
most sensitive, deeply shy person
and she told him, "I'm not
after anything, Brian. So don't
feel you have to sleep with me.
I just like coming around."
He didn't like women
though he had hundreds of them
so she stopped coming round.
Her mother bought her a pram

to push the baby in
She was studying the guitar
an hour a day
That's all.

Hearts

After we've played a noble scene
Where no one is blamed and each
Takes the guilt for not loving enough,
You would think we would break up then and there.

We feel so fine and mature toward each other,
We could cry on the couch like the Idiot
In sympathy for everyone's point of view.

But after we've played our noble scene,
The empathy generates so much lust
That unfortunately, we patch it up
And two weeks later the real cut-throat stuff begins.

September Sundown

As long as the sun's up you are optimistic
A silence occupies the bedroom
Tomato plants in the garden—Indian summer

      The earnest boy with a face like an olive
rides his bike in circles in front of his stoop
working out the terrible thing

      The idler who died in his room all morning, goes out
for a walk
Everyone is glad to be moving
                    like dogs who chase after a stick
The soccer players come kicking straight from work
The sun is weaker over Central Park
Runners, dogwalkers, already the silver body

      is seen above the ballfield
      on a pallid blue sky . The sodium lamps
      light up one by one
          along the path by the lake. Drivers
          notice the lamps challenging the sun,
          and reach for their headlights, to be
          on the safe side

Stubborn hour that won't make up its mind

                  You will follow the sun
as if it were kissing you personally, you will feel kissed
and happy and depressed until the last niggardly change of
daylight falls across your hands   like a farmer in the
middle ages   then you'll go and sit inside in the dark
grow accustomed to it

Men come home from work with the *New York Post* in their arms
playing father to a newspaper
                                    Women run for buses
as if expecting sudden rain   to wash away their dinner dates

        Indian Summer, a good time to make plans.
When the sun goes down everybody feels alone

In the Dentist's Chair

Here I sit in my dentist's chair,
My eyelids shut against the light;
They say that any moment can yield delight
if you will only look at it bare.

I wish I had the knack.
My mind is tired and young.
I can barely turn over my tongue
As she scrapes away the plaque.

It is November, 4:35, and already night.
A smear of sunset crosses the trees like a far-off scream.
The workmen are warming their hands on the steam
and drinking coffee, under a green traffic light.

I could be one of those workmen…
Well, so what?
You could be a baron, an old porter, but you're not.
Don't let's drool sentimentally over them.

Through a plate glass window I see Central Park;
My head is groggy with fatigue;
Muzak seguês from "Hey Jude" to Edvard Grieg.
The Christmas shoppers rush home in the dark.

"Open your mouth?" Doctor Anna's voice interrupts
Distantly, like an upstairs opera singer practicing scales.
I widen my mouth. She leans her female
Body over mine, brushing up.

I imagine throwing my arms around her
And pulling her down to my chest.
Nothing so drastic as sex undressed;
I'm too supine here to be anything but a nuzzler.

Why muddy this delicacy with pornography?
I'm content to smell her cocoanut soap,
The blue nose-mask so close I can reach up
And touch it with a baby's hand and see

Me reflected in her brown eyes,
Helpless and tiny.
Her Indonesian concentration, skin so shiny…
If only she would look at me once with surprise!

She must think me the least of her patients.
I forget to keep my mouth open wide
And irregularly neglect the four roads to gum pride—
The floss, the brush, the red dye and the Stimudents.

"Now let me see how you brush," she directs me,
And hands me a brush as though I were a child.
I wriggle the bristles fast and wild,
Eager to fail and have her correct me.

"You must make circular motions—Here,"
Anna brushes me; "and don't forget *backs* of the teeth.
Run your tongue underneath.
You feel how rough it is there?

Your tongue is your most reliable guide."
I poke around those neglected interiors
That taste as though I had eaten cinders
From Krakatoa, and dust from a landslide.

This tongue I carry everywhere with me,
I could be using constantly to ferret little nooks
Which the brush has overlooked!
Only I know I won't. I'm lazy.

Besides, I feel I've made enough concessions.
Let my teeth fall into rags!

I won't become their slaves. And if she nags
Me any more, I'll tell them what I think of their profession.

Fanatical mechanics with their self-righteous airs—
Anti-Communists of the mouth, waging Holy War on plaque,
I wouldn't be surprised if it were all a quack!
And a century from now, some bright Lavoisier

Will come along and prove
That plaque was an illusion, like phlogiston.
—Calm down, you're begging the question.
It's your reflex perversity you so love—

That habit of cranky refusal;
I've lived with it so long,
Like a favorite opinion one later learned was wrong
But can't help lapsing into its espousal.

How strange how each of us resists the good,
In this or that, for spite. Some deny
Their flesh or stay in jobs that suck them dry,
While I cling to bad teeth and bachelorhood.

Okay, shut up. Pay attention to the office.
There's the glaring lamp, and on the wall
Laminated certificates from dental school:
Academy of Implants, Department of Naval Service,

A Seminar in Dallas—most are Doctor Klein's.
A few are Anna's, backed with plastic or plywood.
They'd laminate their toe-dirt if they could.
Then there's that "painting"—an abstract design

Of mountains, like teeth, to cover a raw edge.
Stay focused outside. Outside, a bird's wing
Flittering; flying to keep from shivering.
The magazines I'll never get to on the window ledge;

The bird in the tree the needle in the gums,
A dry tickling, need to swallow,
The gurgling faucet at my elbow,
My jaws held open with her thumbs…

She nicked me and apologized.
The cut's not painful enough
To blot out everything but itself.
Present can't fill me; still room to fantasize,

Mind rolling back somewhere. Where is it?
Oh yes. The anatomy lesson. How easily
A knife cuts through men's flesh. We
Were being taken through the dissecting room on a visit.

Glenn was anxious to show off his cadaver.
The man's skin had turned olive-green
And rubbery like boiled chicken, and his penis leaned
Handsomely large to one side, awaiting the cleaver.

"Look at this!" another medical student yelled
From two tables down. They pressed around him.
He had struck upon a surgical pin
In his corpse's kneecap, which held

The joints in place. "Keep cutting!"
Someone said, "Let's see the rest."
The scalpel slid as into an overdone roast.
The unresisting muscles parted, exhibiting

A shiver of aluminum. They were spellbound,
As if they'd come upon a will that named them heirs.
"Whoever did it knew his stuff," I heard one swear.
"It must have been a war-time wound!"

I keep returning to that morbid scene—
What's wrong with me tonight? *What's bugging you?*

What are you feeling? A little blue,
I guess. A little down. Melancholy, serene

Like the world in its final hour,
When Matter gives off a modest blush,
The last vital, grey flush on the backs of fish
Flopping in ice. And the gloomy water-tower;

The boulevards in their Viennese decline;
The melon-colored streets at daybreak, looking over-ripe;
Gusts from the river; the broken water-pipes
Flooding the sidewalks with immaculate design.

All of it studied, decomposed, composed, mad:
A manginess more ordered than great art;
I love this state of mind that lets me see each thing apart.
My one last wish is to remain even and sad.

If only I could stay this way forever
Looking calmly out at the plate glass,
I could put up with the coldness and the loss
And be happy knowing I'd be happy—never.

But is that true? Why do I keep
Saying I want to be sad, merely because I
Am? You'll end up making a virtue of every sigh,
And think each letdown is helping you grow deep!

This aesthetics of sadness is a pain in the ass!
There must be something better than this tepid remake,
The cold enjoyment men of introspection take
In re-imagining the world brick by brick as it is.

I want more! One major passion,
And all my meditations can jump out the window.
Make me happy, God; I'll take the risk of being shallow.
I want to kiss the damp earth like a Russian!

Admit it: I'm disappointed. Horrible.
I had expected more. It's all too bland.
(So why is this so hard to understand?
You wanted more, and now you're miserable.)

The girl who charmed me with her feverish effervescence
Is getting married to a walking librium pill.
She who loved large gestures, loved me until
She gave way to an itch for evanescence.

The sorcery of disappearing love
Always distresses and arouses me.
But in fact it is no mystery.
Any judge of character can tell when someone's about to leave.

Then disappointment is all one's fault? You mean,
if I had judged the beloved right on target,
Without fantasies, there'd be no reason to be upset,
Feel rejected or angry at the parting scene?

I've judged intimates correctly and still felt done in.
Foreknowledge and disappointment run on separate tracks.
What's so good about predicting the crumbling from the cracks?
In the end would I feel any less chagrined?

It's not as if I've been betrayed at every turn.
People have loved me, licked me with their warm fidelity.
In some funny way none of it touches me.
I'm still here playing solitaire on the mind's green lawn.

"Ah, tomorrow you'll feel better. You're just spent.
You've run around all week, giving orders, alert,
And you come here to a chair where you're forced to be inert:
Of course you're set upon by every stray lament!

All the urges you'd suppressed to get your work done,
They're jumping up and throwing their weight around.

A good night's sleep, and you'll feel much more sound."
Despair and Optimism—see how they run.

I get tired chasing them. Neither is me.
Giving myself pep talks, perking up the troops,
And allowing myself an occasional day-off to mope.
Is there any *me* beyond this rapid change of strategy?

"Rinse out please." I spit
Surprising embryos of blood into a suction cup;
I can't keep saliva from dribbling up
My face, I'm turning into a drooling idiot.

I bend and rinse again for good measure.
My stomach almost gags on the taste
Of that green, gritty, peppermint polishing paste.
She watches with what I imagine to be displeasure.

"Today was only a scraping and a cleaning
To remove the pileup. You had plenty of tartar,"
She starts to scold me. The door is ajar
And, tanned from a conference in Texas, Klein comes in gleaming.

"How's my boy doing?" Anna falls silent.
He is the Jove of the office, she his assistant.
She does the routine work, he the tricky implants.
"You look as if you've been in an accident,"

Klein laughs. This is his idea of professional wit.
"How are you coming along?"
I try to speak but my mouth is still all tongue.
"It looks all right," says Anna, seeing fit

To shelter me from the father's wrath—
Or is it to protect herself? In any case,
She has given me a moment's grace
Before he can unearth the guilty truth.

"Let's see his X-rays. I'm just curious...
Hm. Not bad for cavities. How about the gums?"
He lifts my lip up with his thumbs.
"You call this—'all right'?" Klein is furious.

"Those gums look awfully beefy!
We're gonna have to do better than that!
You're flirting with periodontitis, friend—gum rot.
You'll have to play ball with us or face surgery.

"We can't do it all for you, hold your hand,
We can't go to your house every morning."
His face is breaking out in hives of warning.
Next he remembers to bully the good Anna.

"These X-rays are too cloudy. Oh, they're legible
But not razor-sharp. Lacking in contour."
And he explains his point with a metaphor
From baseball: "Why go for a single

When you can hit the ball out of the park?"
Which probably means nothing to this Indonesian.
Still, I understand his need to rub it in:
A perfectionist making others toe the mark.

In this, Klein is gross caricature of me:
The lifelong insecurity of Ivy League men
Who have passed all exams, and then
Keep wheedling higher grades from sluggish humanity.

She's close to tears—am I imagining that?
Like a child who's scolded and feels
A sore throat coming on, she conceals
Her swallows while he explains the art.

Her eyes are dark and now she moves her glance
To the cool white counter and the swabs,

To the cupful of scissors, as one day she might stab
Her all-knowing boss in the forehead in a trance.

Klein fails to understand he has gone too far.
I am watching them both, when suddenly,
She reaches for a toothbrush and gives it to me.
A second later, as if by signal, he is out the door.

A new toothbrush, a gift of the management
Which delights me, though the cynic thinks from habit:
"At these prices they can afford it."
I put on my overcoat, and wave goodbye to the arrangements.

The Last Slow Days of Summer

"BE YOUR OWN MASTER!" says the Vedanta Society sign.
Why not?…In the park
Some clouds roll over me like Greenland on a map.
If I wanted to I could imagine I was flying over
The Greenland coast and gazing down at the white fjords.
Instead I'm lying on the grass, listening to city sounds.
They come to me in three-dimensional form,
Like a loaf of Wonder Bread. Baby carriages squeak
Near the middle. Cars humming through Central Park,
Somewhere near the back of the loaf.
What sound would be the end-piece, the round brown sliver?
The unzipping of airline bags.
Or a glove thwacked
By a rookie pitcher who falls apart
In the eighth inning. The manager takes the ball silently,
Like a man who has eaten a full loaf of bread
And has a stomach pain. Don't glamorize silence.
There is nothing profound about quiet, it is usually
Only the universe holding its stomach.

Delmore Schwartz must have been a great talker.
They say he put most of his talent into his life
But I don't know, I think his prose is pretty great;
He made a better storywriter than a poet.
I could write a thousand-page biography
Propounding that stance, and interview all the old rummy
Critics who are powerful now;
They would let their hair down about Delmore,
And the final crackup.
The reason I'm thinking of Delmore Schwartz is that
he wrote a poem about city parks. And it wasn't that successful,
It went on for about twelve pages, but I admired him
For writing a poem with so little point,
And so much prosy description. I think he was trying to

Eulogize normal middle-class happiness on a Sunday afternoon,
And how he felt out of it. But that wouldn't have
Taken twelve pages...He was probably being ironic
About the people's happiness, and secretly thought
They weren't happy. He wrote it about the same time
Robert Moses was carving out his parks empire
By forcing the Long Island millionaires to give up their privacy
So that the middle class could get to the beach.
Of course it was also supposed to benefit
The poor slum-dwellers, but how many of them
Ever made it to Sunken Meadows?
Or Jones Beach?

What's strange about parks—innocent greenery—
Is that no one ever suspected them to ruin New York.
Yet what finally gutted the city were the parkways
Moses built, slashed through all five boroughs
Quiet lower-middle-class neighborhoods bulldozed
For cars to get to the picnic grounds faster,
Or the Hamptons—
A life of paperwork capped by a summer home.
But I can't blame them: I'd like a summer home myself!
I don't really believe New York is dying, no more than
The universe is dying. I have no stake in seeing
This poem end pessimistically.
I'd like to leave people with a good feeling.

Robert Moses, Delmore Schwartz.
Two ambitious Jews, like myself.
They tried to be their own masters...
It's hard to imagine New York going under
on a slow summer day like today
Without even a loud noise to mark it
Like the Empire State Building keeling over
And everyone running to the scene of default.
The helicopters will be standing by,
Ready to take us to Greenland.

A special airlift for poetic men of letters,
A jumbo Boeing crammed to the teeth,
And you can't get in if your name isn't
Listed in Poets and Writers Directory.
"So long, New York School of Poets!"
I'll stay behind, tending the weeds
And sleeping in deserted Central Park.
Soon I'll be hearing about the Godthaab School:
Their seemingly infinite talent for "chatty brilliance,"
Buddhism, and marathon readings.
I'll shake my head and sigh: What are
Anne and Michael doing now?
How was this year's big Halloween party,
Or do they even celebrate Halloween in Greenland?
Maybe they're into solstice holidays, like Midsummer Night.

The Truth That Hurts

I

Funny how when I think back now
to how I was at college, I can't
Distinguish me from all the rest;
We're sitting down at Rikers,
With one white counter snaking
Through the stools,
Eavesdropping on the loud girl telling
About her suicide attempt with razors
To her embarrassed friend.
It sounded too familiar.
Suicide was like a garden of spices
For the blind, that we visited
From time to time with our eyes
Open, sampling the air.

Our lives, like the black-and-white
Films we could never resist,
Were grainy, harsh as sixteen millimeter
Blown up to thirty-five.
We liked it that way: austere.
But no—we wanted more, we never
Tired of saying it; and the more was
Each other that we could tell this to.
We told each other all.
Those were the days we had such an itch
To confide, and what hurt most seemed truest.
Only a confidence could arouse
The acrid precise, like the smell
Of a lit match held between two sets of eyes.
Time stops when you say what
You thought you never could,
And here you are still breathing like a courtier at the Borgias.

Now I begin to pick me out a bit:
I was the one who came from Brooklyn slums,
And never wanted my roommates to forget it.
But they took me in without making a fuss
About social class, which chagrined me.
I fell in with the literary set,
And by junior year I'd gotten my desk
At the college magazine, *Columbia Review*,
With my own swivel-chair that I loved
moving round in without standing up.
That was the game: to answer the phone like
A paraplegic wheeling over to behind the desk:
"Hello? Review!"

In my senior year I was Editor-in-chief.
In the bottom drawers of my desk I'd find
Chocolate pudding dishes from the lunchroom,
That I traced to a bearded sophomore poet
Who had horrible broken front teeth
And a demented way of not looking at you
While singing throaty countertenor madrigals.
He also wrote epic poems about
Jewish cemeteries. One day I caught him:
Burst in as he was applying
A spoonful of pudding to his beard.
Bashful smile (relieved at being caught?)
The others were crazier.
And so I flourished.

II

Jon and I were sitting on the grass
Behind the Metropolitan Museum;
He asked me didn't I mind the loss
Of Nature, and the separation
Between cities and lakes trees brooks?
Didn't I mind the concrete everywhere?
I said I loved it; Loss was for the academics.

He took my narrowness for courage.
That was my way: I backed up prejudices strong.
People with more culture than I
Were shaken. Years later, they quoted
These statements back to me as turning-points
In their lives, and I was appalled.
Did I say that bunk? What provincialism.
Nevertheless I was pleased.

Always pleased to make an impression on people.
Arrogance trumps uncertainty; I talked my way
Into jobs I knew nothing about, because
Some knew even less.
When push comes to shove, an insight
Can be teased from a particular;
And wisdom, approached as a tonal problem,
Reduced to a set of dots and reproduced.

III

I give my opinions out for a fee now.
A roving consultant, I go on nerve,
Till one day, at a rural university
Whose new glass study center is sunk in snow
I see myself ponderously crossing a windy campus
After a faculty luncheon that's bloated me
And Professor DuB—is taking me by the arm;
Yes I'll talk my head off, must give them a good show,
While all I'm thinking is
The turkey strand between my teeth, if I could only work it out,
And my feet getting frozen in the snow.
My audience stirs as I walk through the door.
I see the podium of rich blonde wood,
Oh, and the automatic blackboard-screen
That disappears at the push of a button!

The walls are *art brut* modern, fired brick,
And the floors made with grey slats of concrete

That a prisoner could tear his hands on for centuries.
I stare from the pit at the tilted red aisles, a steep lookup
To the top row. No clock in back.
I pace. I talk. I cry. I'm brilliant
And the crowd laughs. I make it into a song
As I go along, I make up my little song:
A little audacity, a little skepticism
And real-life anecdotes that warm the house.
Always pleased to have an effect on people.
Only now they want to know
Where I got my facts.

"You still haven't answered my question,"
Taunts the lanky young man in the brown corduroy jacket
In the next to the last row, and whatever I say
Makes him slump even further in his seat.
"I don't care for your constant use of the masculine gender,"
A woman in front objects.— "Give us more details!"—
"How can we trust you when you're not specific enough?"

If I keep still their anger will go away.
For starters I'll agree: yes, well
The problem *is* complex
And we must break for snack.
But the room stays very tense.
And there's nothing I can do to remove it,
Their resentment comes from a deeper source,
They want answers for their lives,
There is nothing I can do.

IV

"You want people to adore you,"
Said my last girlfriend, analyzing our breakup.
"You try to get people to adore you
And people oblige (they do when you make that
Need clear enough, that's why you're successful);
But you keep them at a distance when it comes to love

Because you can't give back equal love.
Oh—you're incredibly supportive;
But that supportiveness is the expression
Of your guilt for not being able to love them.
I'm not saying you couldn't love anyone,
But it's you who thinks that you can't,
Doubts that you can, so you help people instead.
By being everyone's support, it's also a way
To stay in command.

"Actually there's nothing wrong with wanting Adoration
And Power. They're great," she said.
"It's your guilty conscience that spoils it.
Why are you so guilty? Your guilt's what muddies everything."

I agreed; it was probably true.
"And that's another thing," she went on;
"You're willing to admit criticism of yourself,
But you do it just to take the credit for openness,
And it stays on a purely verbal level.
You don't really take it into yourself.
You only like the pose of confessing
Wrongdoing; you like it so much that it
Completely bypasses your heart.
You think you're perfect; that's your problem."

That's not so, I said.
Sometimes I take criticism to heart
And I've let myself be changed by it.
There are times when I'm not defensive.
There are also certainly other times when I am.

"That's my final point!" she cried.
"My final point is that you qualify everything!
Your favorite way of countering criticism
Is to say: 'Well to some extent yes, not always.'
That's how you deaden the truth that hurts."

The Daily Round

to Mandelstam

Last cup of coffee,
Go slowly through the day
Pick up the laundry on the way home from work
Walk slowly through the grimy streets
This is your last chance to see this life

See how the sunlight beats against the curtains
Trying to force its way in
Defeated by a thin green rag,
Its knuckles weaken and it falls to the cement
I can watch them for hours
Leaning on my pillow
Without lifting a finger to help

My God, how I love this world

Remember that the sun is yellow
No matter what they try to tell you
Remember times of peace
When the Brillo Pad drools
Against a warm dish
Remember that you said, "But I love
This poor earth, because I have not seen another"
Remember how the sky is grey or pink or black
And that her hair falls straight across her back
When you hear the passkey turning in the lock.

PART 3
UNCOLLECTED POEMS

Clearing A Space

I am clearing the space for a lover
To enter my life, I am clearing off a big space.
Today when I went bicycling I saw
On the grass one pair of lovers after another.
They were lying on each other, like rugs or fur coats
And all you could see was the shaggy mane of a redhead
Or the lips a boy pressed down on his girl
While their limbs held chastely still.

I walked my bicycle past them, thinking
For a moment of every lover I'd enjoyed
And when none of them made my heart sink,
And when I experienced no pain,
Then I knew I was free of them
And that I was clearing a new space
As big as my life, as big as the pasture
The lovers were linked on.

     I am preparing a space for the loved one:
I know what she looks like already.
She looks like the dark-haired girl in blue
I only saw for a second before her Hispanic lover
                         covered her.
Then, when I circled back on my bike, she was on top.
But I rode on because my time will come
And meanwhile I am preparing a space,
I am cutting the grass for the loved one to walk on;
I am cleaning my heart, making my thoughts unrancorous,
Learning to be patient.
And if it should prove to be in the end
Not a woman, not a human lover entering after all,
But something fuller and sadder, like the world,
Like God, I will only say I suspected it all along.

The Japanophiles

When she was young, in her twenties, she had gone to Japan.
She had studied Noh, and taken a Japanese lover.
I can imagine him
with sloping muscles, hairless chest, an earnest face
that squinted when the window shade was drawn.
She hungers for that Japanese type now: something about
the way they made love, something he taught her
about silences, engrossment, the going-under
that she tried to bring back with her to the States.
Vain about her gift for sexuality,
she let herself be backup love for well-known
writers, painters, publishers, Powers;
she did it open-eyed, unjealous of their wives,
living off crouton bits of love and free-lance work,
a cultivated stylish woman approaching thirty-eight.
Depressed as she so often is, her lowered head, her neck
resemble a geisha's in an Utamaro print, gracefully waiting
behind a mosquito net.

I come by her apartment every so often.
We talk about Japanese things.
I, also a Japanophile, claim it is a most unhappy culture,
obsessed with retrospective glance, the irretrievable,
a fatalism in the prose and brush. Perhaps
permissive childhoods, doting grandparents,
followed by too-strict schooling, conspire to make them
bound-up, tied in knots, thinking of the past
as a golden age. I may not have the social science right
but the fact remains their art is melancholy,
which is why I love it. No accident Kawabata
chose *Beauty and Sadness*
for the title of his last novel.

She disagrees. "No, you don't understand,
you are exaggerating the transience theme,
the cherry blossoms and so on. That's a cliché.
What foreigners tend to overlook in Japanese art,
but what I learned when I was over there,
is that they treat the moment like a synapse:
all they will speak about is just-before
and just-after,
but there is no people better able to block out
everything but the immediate, these four walls—
which is why they are so good at sex.
Take Saikaku. They've none of that Western shame
about sexual appetite, or that post-coital letdown
(which I have never understood myself,
though witnessed it in men often enough).
The Meiji era spoiled some of that, true, with its
Westernizing drive, but if you go back to before the Meiji…"

We both have our Japan.
Mine is elegiac, hers ecstatic.
I cannot help but think she pays
for that ecstasy: transfigured by sublimity's ghost,
her works are scattered, ambitious but diffuse,
she lacks a practical footing in the world,
while in her mind persists, with clarity and taste,
a room of lust.
She's kept alive her vision of pure sensual space
that paradoxically ties her to depression
and all the shocks from bruising ordinary life,
to which she must present her résumés still,
with sore availability.

No doubt we are both right. Or wrong.
Long ago I settled for a workmanlike,
productive, stoic life, in which

the concept of bliss is meaningless.
Maybe I fear her capacities.
                                   I would almost
step forward and offer myself as a lover,
but I see in her eyes that my body is all wrong,
too hairy and soft, she would prefer
a man who knew more silences—
while I too have my exotic fantasies.

Just to Spoil Everything

I won't call up first, I'll just ring your bell
out of left field and walk in:
just because you told me
we were not supposed to see each other
until you said it was all right to do so,
until you felt less hysterical
(or whatever your crazy excuse was).
But I'm going over to your apartment house
right now, while you're waiting for some old boyfriend
for tea, just to spoil everything.
I'll rush in by surprise,
sit in your rocking chair
and say nothing, don't expect a scene.
Perhaps I won't even take off my overcoat
with the orange knit scarf you gave me for Christmas.
My scarf will glint reproachfully at you.
I'll show you how unworldly I can be!
Because I want to make a mess of things,
of that fond poetic tender last impression
you would like to keep of me.

The Second Marriage

In the second marriage they indulge themselves,
Give lots of dinner parties, entertain,
Knowing the price of too much symbiosis.
Weekends they play, dress down; they share
The affectation of décolletage:
Her plunging tunic, his designer shirt
Unbuttoned to the waist, grey chest hairs.
And grass on Sunday mornings, snacks in bed.
Demonstrative in public: sitting on his lap
She rubs the curly hair behind his ear,
While they go right on talking to their friends.

All shortages of that first, Puritan marriage
Straight out of college, serious and dour,
Are now corrected Epicurean-style.
They buy each other fancy gifts (why not?
They both are pulling in good salaries):
Twin bicycles, cases of Beaujolais,
A brownstone where they can put up
Their twenty-something kids from the first marriage.

These offspring drift in pallidly:
The boy's a washed-out longhair into rock,
The girl a tomboy who just likes to hike.
They seem unsure in this so-sensuous crowd;
Perhaps they both take after the dour parent
Who was left behind. The boy makes himself useful
Changing discs, hiding by the speakers.
He finds this sybaritic spectacle revolting, but
"Maybe they're right. They all have such conviction.
Maybe this time I'll get it if I watch...."

And then, the invitation's always there
To take advantage of their generosity,

The private screenings of old Fred Astaires,
The crowd with dinner dishes on their laps,
Applauding each dance climax. Between reels,
The Minnie Mouse collection on the mantel,
And afterwards some coffee, chocolate mousse.
These people know exactly what they want.
The second marriage has to work:
It lasts 'til Death.

For Coffee

The editor invited me for coffee
after his magazine took one of my poems.
He lived in one of those rambling West End apartments
that doubled back on itself, with double doors
and stacks of review books unopened,
and bills on the dining room table.

He'd just shown me in when the phone rang.
"Excuse me," he said and went into the next room.
I snooped around his bookcase. Underneath
some journals was a personal letter I could
just barely make out: "Words are useless at a time
like this. Please call if there is something we can do."
I almost moved the pile to read the rest,
but it was clear enough, someone had died.
That might explain his voice each time we'd spoken:
heavy and tired, deep-piled with meaning
beyond the simple businesslike exchange.
                              "Sorry to keep you waiting,"
he said, steering me into the kitchen
where he ground coffee in a French machine.
"My children will be home soon.
I've got to start their dinner—my wife died recently."

                              I nodded.
That I showed no surprise seemed possibly rude,
yet I did not want to make too much of it;
after all, I'd just met him. He looked no more
than forty-five, it must have hit him hard.
                              "What of?" I asked.
"Cancer." And he laughed. (What was the joke?)
"'Cancer,' said the man lighting a cigarette,"
he mocked himself, shaking the match flame out.
"How old was she?"

"Just turned forty. She was an artist. Sculptor.
Actually, more a potter," he emended,
as if to falsify her after death in any way
might bring bad luck.
"She laughed a lot. We all knew it was coming.
But still, no matter how much you prepare...."

I shook my head in understanding, it all
seemed possible and true.
I looked around the kitchen at the children's artwork
pinned on the refrigerator with magnetic bars:
colored sailboats, a purple horse,
stick figures of a family held in place,
nothing unusual; and on the other wall
a large rough valentine on yellow drawing paper—
"We love you Mommy!
To the best best Mommy in the whole wide world"—
lettered more desperately than usual.

Venetian Silences

I came late into Venice my first time, and surrendered
to those hotel pilot-fish who wait outside the train.
"You want a room? I take you."—"Yes, why not?"
"All three together?" "What three?" I asked,
and turned to see two girls, Americans,
leaning on knapsacks, with sun-scarred, sullen faces.
"No, I'm alone." The two pushed past me,
asking in Italian: "How much for a double?"
"Cheap. Few dollars," shrugged the grey-haired guide,
wearing a visored captain's cap logoed "Hotel Fortuna."
They grumbled and boarded the boat.
I wondered if they might be lovers.
Probably not. They seemed resentful toward
the world, but not each other.

                      The ferry boat took off:
I leaned over the railing, laughing as we rolled by Venice,
incredulous at the silliness of that fantastic movie set:
Stone palaces bobbing in the sea, next to restaurants
brashly canopied, and a rosy Turner sunset off the starboard.
It was every bit as nutty as I'd hoped.
I proudly joined the legions of gullible tourists
who had fallen for this mirage: they'd never build
a city so impractical, improbable and wet.

We debarked at Accademia, and were led
through that dramatic spacious square
to a narrow canal filled with fresh green paint
(the natives called it water). Tied up near the bridge
was a floating grocery store, a gondola
packed with eggplant and bananas.
Our feet exploded like tap shoes on the paving stones.
No one spoke, the girls walked far ahead,
as if to discourage one from getting ideas.

The lobby of the small Hotel Fortuna
had tiled black floors smelling of ammonia.
The rooms surrounded a court on all four sides
and in the marbled center stood a hotel desk.
I let the girls go first, then I approached the clerk.
He was twenty-three or so, indoor-pallid and ironic,
with that excess of intelligence sometimes found
spilling from minor functionaries,
like foam from a boiling pot of spaghetti.
"How many days will you stay?" he asked
in English. A week, I thought.
He had only a back room to give me,
without much sun, but maybe in a few days
something better would come free.
We went upstairs to see the floppy bed, soft
with a white chenille cover, a light-switch
that looked like a fat water bug by the headboard.
The walls, dark purple, slanted to a gabled roof.
A washstand near the window, from which one
might see a triangle of stars and stone.
I nodded: this would do fine. He gently smiled,
and left me alone.
                    In this reserved exchange,
there seemed a lilt, a subtle bond of understanding.

I lay on my bed, wondering if I had imagined
this affinity. To find a Hamlet under every hotel clerk
was to colonize people for my own narratives.
Perhaps what I had taken for sensitivity
was only his hesitancy in speaking English.
I suddenly felt restless to take in Venice.
As I descended the stairs, I noticed that he
put away a thick book on hearing my footsteps.
His face went from preoccupied to keen
as I approached the desk. "Do you have
a map of Venice?"—"We do," he said
and fished one assiduously from the desk.

I leaned over to glimpse the title of the book,
but it was covered up.
"What were you reading just now?" I asked.
He blushed. I thought it might be something
sexy, I hadn't meant to catch him in the act,
and now he looked about uneasily for rescue,
stalling. "A novel," he said finally.
"I figured that. But what's its name?"
 "*Oblomov.*" He took the red and gold-gilt book
by Goncharov out of the drawer as proof.
"It's one of my favorite novels!" I cried.
"Yes, I am enjoying it so far." He said he liked
Lermontov even more—*A Hero of Our Time.*
Lermontov, another favorite of mine.

It seemed that every month
he went down to the kiosk in the square
and bought potluck the latest Classic:
a cheaply priced edition, mostly nineteenth century,
Balzac, Jane Austen, Henry James, Hardy.
And some were disappointing. But still
he took his chances, and this Goncharov he liked.
I was so happy to find another lover of classics
that I asked him to go down the entire list
of which books he liked and didn't like,
to see if our tastes concurred. Mostly they did.
We carried on for fifteen amiable minutes
a conversation all in proper nouns,
handshakes and wrinkled noses—grammar dismissed,
no verbs, only the glorious names of geniuses
and their works, until someone came by
and wanted to know how to change Travelers Checks.

Then I went out for my walk, crossed bridges,
ate mediocre pizza, wandered through
echoing deserted piazzas with tourist-trap cafés,
saw two bands playing imperturbably across

from one another, passed sailors and other nomads
like myself, none of us certain what we were
supposed to do with the long albino night.

                        Coming home mildly drunk,
hugging the walls along my narrow street,
afraid of pitching into the canal, and trying
to silence my murderer's tap shoes,
I suddenly felt less alone, thinking of how
I would greet the hotel clerk who read.
"G'night, Giorgio," I said on my way upstairs
and he waved and yawned good night.

                   He must be the night clerk too,
I thought, to be working the desk so late.
But in the morning he was there as well,
in dark blue suit and tie. Perhaps he was
their only clerk. No wonder he looked so sallow.
The two American girls were already seated
in the dining room, eating breakfast,
going through tourist booklets. I nodded.
They were sulky as usual, or should I say
the thin one was, and the large-boned one
was trying to follow suit. "Mary?" she called
to her friend, but the thin, hatchet-faced Mary
kept reading, as irritated as one could look
without crossing over into outright anger.
I sensed the chubby one would have
happily essayed a smile to the other diners,
if only Mary would give her the go-ahead.

That day I went walking, as I would each morning,
through the curved streets, museums, the Piazza
San Marco, took the vaporetto to Lido, mostly
wandered the working-class quarter behind Accademia,
watching Italian fathers play with their children
so easily it ruffled my heart. I spied on packs of

teenage girls and boys wearing tight V-necks
meeting in the square, as if by happy accident.
I saw archways painted with voting slogans
in green paint for Fascists, in red for the Left;
and once, coming upon an old back street
where two canals met, I stopped and listened
to the lurch of water gurgling against the locks,
stared at a jam-up of timber and shattered boat,
mesmerized by the silence and sun-splashed houses
painted apricot and grey, till from one of the villas
came an ear-splitting amplified blues guitar band.

For days I spoke to no one, nourishing solitude,
sharpening my reticence like a blade, even
pointing and miming to shopkeepers. I offered money
silently, took my change, and in the sundrenched strolls
of late afternoon, became a little unbalanced
from bottled-up ecstasy and voices in my head,
lyrically sloshing about like saliva.
For some stupid reason, maybe to test myself,
don't ask me why, I'd made a vow
to speak to no one in Venice—allowing myself
just one exception, the hotel clerk.

Each day we'd have one conversation,
usually after breakfast. He'd listen to my peripatetic reports
with bleary skeptical eyes. Nothing bored him more
than Venice, its "eternal beauty" got on his nerves.
He seemed disappointed that I loved it so,
proving I had no more taste than all the others.
To him Venice was a prison:
in winter it showed its true nature,
grim. The monotonous fog, the stones, the pea-green sea,
the damp canal winds cutting through your skin—
a bad place to be poor. To pay for law school
he scrounged up any job, waiter, usher at La Fenice,
but jobs were scarce, he had to wait for hotel season

to begin to make some money. Winters he starved.
Summers he worked, *worked*, from six in the morning
till midnight at the hotel. What kind of life was that?
When he finished his degree he would clear out of Venice.
"Where to?" I asked. Maybe America, he had a friend
in Chicago, maybe Trieste where he had another friend.
'Trieste," I sighed, "Italo Svevo's town!"
"Yes, *Confessions of Zeno*. A very good book."
"One of my all-time favorites," I enthused.
"Trieste…. I would like some day to live in Trieste,"
he repeated pensively, liking the sound of the name.
"It's quite close, isn't it?"
"Only a boat-ride away," he muttered sadly,
as if it were completely beyond his powers.

I walked all day, and came back after ten,
my legs having given out. By the church was a cantina.
The stars put on a show in the night sky
like a planetarium doming the piazza.
There was one little breeze.
As I stumbled toward an empty table outside
I saw the two girls and my Italian Oblomov
having a drink.
                          This shocked me.
I realized from his attentive courtly manner
he was trying to make the skinny one.
He looked up suddenly and seeing me, blushed,
while she seemed peeved, as if my presence
might spoil everything. All three invited me
to join them, which I did.
I wanted to watch him operate.
Unfortunately, no sooner had I pulled up a chair
than he started making general remarks
in elaborate circumvention of the evening's purpose;
and I sensed him underneath apologizing to me.

In fact I did think less of him. Only the other day

he'd asked me what I thought of the two girls,
and I said they struck me as drab and ignorant
and he seemed to agree. I felt betrayed,
not only by his minor lie, but more so by my own
naivete, that part of me that never understands
how other people are pairing behind my back.
My throat swelled up, the way it does from fear.
Meanwhile, the other girl started to come alive,
and asked me what I did. I realized that moment
I was going to have to break my fast of speech,
which no one knew about in any case;
it would have been too rude not to reply.
I said I was a writer, and she seemed impressed.
She had once kept a diary for three months,
but she quit because the whole thing made her sick.
I might have asked her how it made her sick
or turned this opening into a flirtation,
but flirting seemed beyond my parched reflexes.
Nevertheless, I found it easy to hold forth—
I found I had a hunger to be heard.
The evening ended two drinks later with
a hot political fight, in which the angry Mary
took on everything I said.
I was glad to lock horns with her, while
Oblomov watched with downcast fascination.

The next morning I got up late.
The cleaning women had taken over the stairs
with their mops and ammonia, their loud voices
ruling the hotel, the guests feeling like interlopers.
I crept downstairs over a damp-mopped floor,
and was about to slip out when my friend Giorgio
called to me. He had found me another room,
much sunnier and larger than the one I had—
of course more expensive, but I could have it
for just a bit more, maybe even the same price.
He seemed embarrassed lest I think

the hotel was trying to milk me.
I knew very well he was doing me a favor,
the only gift he was in a position to bestow.
I wondered too if this might be his way
of making up for last night…But why?
He had done nothing wrong. "How are
our American friends?" I asked mischievously.
"Who?" He seemed genuinely perplexed.
"The two girls, the ones we drank with last night."
"Oh—they checked out this morning."
We climbed the mop-slippery marble steps,
and as we reached the second floor he said,
"I live on this wing myself, it's very nice,
the rooms are bright…" and drifted into
disconcerted silence.
He took out his keys, becoming
a hotel clerk showing someone a room:
arms crossed in front of his chest, patient,
I couldn't bear to see him act that way.
"Fine, I'll take it," I blurted, and moved
my belongings within the hour. A pity:
I'd come to like my somber purple garret,
and this one was so light that it unnerved me.
I could think of nothing to do
but sit on the edge of my bed
and look out at the garden in back
and stare at laundry flapping on the line,
and watch a lizard crawling up the wall.

The Gary Who Loved Schubert

had braces on his teeth
and he said, "Listen to this"
and a funny sickly look came over him
a look I had never seen
in a twelve year old

He held up the jacket photo
of Toscanini conducting
in green—a forest of hands
"Well, what do you think of Schubert?"
I didn't know what to think
Sounded pretty mushy to me

"I would have to hear it again.
What's it called?"
"*The Unfinished Symphony,*" Gary beamed,
but if it was unfinished, what was he so glad about?
I tried to imagine a really big ending for it
This all took place in his bedroom

the one and only time
I visited my classmate Gary's house
How envious I was
of his stereo speakers
and the dreamy burden that clouded his eyes
the burden of understanding Schubert

The Bright Spot Luncheonette

The owner is a Greek about thirty-five
with glasses and a pasty intelligent face.
He buries himself behind the counter
six days a week, counting newspapers unsold.
Is he so new to this country he thinks
he can save a bundle from a hole in the wall like this?

Last summer he went back to Peloponnesus
to fetch a teenage bride from his village.
The girl is well-built
and has quickly caught on to hip-hugger fashions
and is already pregnant.

Her mother, who lives with them
in a Bronx three-room apartment,
spends hours at the luncheonette
chatting away in vivacious Greek.
Her mother is foxy-looking,
would probably make a better wife for the owner
(I doubt he would agree).

The girl understands no English at all;
she mixes egg creams behind the counter
with downcast dreamy eyes
while seltzer spills over the glass.

Her hips are beginning to spread.

The owner watches me watching her.

Laziness

Look at the sun and close your eyes
You see a pineapple ring, right?
An ant is tangled in my arm hair
Another ant crawls across my back
                    taking its time

Again I'm humbled
Things cling like algae in a mountain lake
    or circumstantial friends, although
I've spent some happy days with them
Swimming to the raft
And patting my belly smoothly
And talking about blue skies

In winter you need to be a bit more clever
You can't act as if you were forever
On a bicycle, laughing and grunting
And pointing: *Look at that big dog!*
Jesus it's hot!

                    Though it's a pity
We can't be loved for our stupidity,
Which stays the largest part of us,
The mumbler that waits for summer
To break through, like bongo drums

Love's Freely Chosen

Each animal's on his own. The llama and the duck
Walk self-absorbed along the coast where two sheep fuck.
The tortoise carries his stone,
Each animal is essentially alone.

The gorilla tries to climb out of the bandstand,
Then realizes he is resting in a hand.
He cries to the lizard, who stares at him frozen
Because love is not coerced bur freely chosen

And she is storing up her heart for a man
With the cold unreachable eyes of an afghan.
So each one waits for a passion worth the sacrifice
While passing up Life like a minor vice.

What's Left in the Pot at the End of the Day?

"He goes up for a three-point layup!
Career-high total in a playoff!"
How do these guys do it?

The murderous-faced bifocaled
game-watcher when I get in his way
and spill some beer on his sleeve
William Carlos Williams: "There's an awful lot
of b-bastards out there"

It's good to be alone after the sports bar
reading a fat English novel past midnight
and thinking about the way my colleague-crush
asked me in Europa Coffee Shop:
"So how are *you* feeling""
while buttoning up her thin brown cardigan
like, Make it quick.
She may've been genuinely interested but
           had a doctor's appointment.

We paid the bill. I still had my chance.
      When you come right down to it,

Feelings don't take very long to tell.

What's left in the pot at the end of the day?
A few kept-in feelings, like spaghetti strings
the Brillo pad missed.

Doing Crossword Puzzles

We hold the magazine across our laps,
a warm spot on our legs, like a pet cat
or child. "What's 'Philippine dwarf?'"
We'll leave that one alone.
"Entombs" could be "buries" or "inurns."
And "Actor Jack" should be "LaRue."
Whoever wrote this puzzle must be old
and mean. "What's 'Nightingale's companion'?"
A *lamp!* Pretty good, eh?
      She nods; she's not impressed.
She won't admit how brilliant I am.
Though it's true she cracked the hardest one:
"External world"—who would have thought, *Nonego*?

My father used to do the Sunday Crosswords
and I never understood why so much effort
for so little practical reward.
Mom wanted him to sell insurance
so he could make more money—
a reasonable request for a breadwinner of six.
He studied the insurance training guides
with their stock euphemisms for Death:
"What if you were to 'fade out of the picture'?"
They stuck in his craw. He never passed
the oral interview part of the exam.
But he finished every crossword in the *Times*.

If you gave me a word-association test
and said "Crossword puzzle—quick!"
I probably would answer "Failure."
It conjures up the obloquy
of newsprint ink and ballpoint leaks
that smear off on the hands, like family life.
Boxes of pedantry where everything fit:

for Pop, completion was a weekly Ph.D.
to dull the pain of genteel poverty,
the way he quoted Latin to fellow clerks:
"How much longer will you abuse our patience,
O Cataline?"

For years I wouldn't go near even Scrabble.
I would escape the family tar.
But Saturday night, we weren't getting along,
wouldn't love each other, wouldn't fight;
we bought the Sunday *Times* and lugged it home.
In moody silence, on the nubby couch,
she took out the crossword and started to fill it in.
I sat beside her, waiting for permission.
"This one is really difficult," she said.
"Want me to take a look at it?" I asked.
"Uhmm," she grunted, neither yes nor no.
"What's 34 Across?"—"It just says
'The Green Wave.'"—"Never heard of it.
I think 'vituperation' is 'abuse.'"
"Does it fit?"—"Sure. Let me have a piece of it."
She slid half of the puzzle on my lap,
as though it were a comforter for chills.
I sagged into my father's frame, my shoulders
suddenly drooping, frail.
I felt near you, O Father, O Cataline!
I'd screwed-up, too. I had failed,
I was ready for the crosswords' consolation.

The Chestnut

One night Tatania met a famous poet
who asked to be taken home.
He was a sweet old drunk but wouldn't listen:
he wanted her to use a chestnut
for a birth control device.
And afterwards she asked about him at parties,
shyly going up to his disciples,
saying, "Tell him I am ready.
I have planted the chestnut inside me."
But the young men leaned against her silently,
mistaking her for a tree.

Poem

the icicles on Afros
settle like tinsel
as the moviegoers stream out:
Is it snowing?
Has it started to snow?
Let's stand here a second and watch.

when you leave a movie theatre
and it is suddenly darker
and the snow's suspended
in a yellow brownout

over the sloshy streets
you might as well throw yourself in the river
but instead you take a walk by the river
and stand gazing at the fog

that lifts you
to the other side of the world

The National Elections

The day after the national elections
when yet another Republican is triumphant
a hurricane floods the road across Central Park
Water sluices over rocks and drain pipes,
forming white shaggy cascades every twenty feet
I stare out my taxi window
A veteran who has seen it all

The cars float toward the East Side
their tires are completely submerged

The next night Belinda holds a restaurant candle
against a black ashtray, and talks about the veins
pulsing just beneath the surface
like energy flashes, and says,
"There are so many things one can't put into words,
don't you agree?"
No, I answer. Everything can be put in words.
Then we go see an old movie *Destination Moon*

The Community Organizer's Wife

For nine years we lived together
marched on picket lines
cold groggy nights
I gave you that zippo lighter admiration
guaranteed even in high winds
to build you up
because God knows
         you needed it
all the time I kept waiting
for you to start nurturing me
developed circles under my eyes
and after nine long years
you tell me
you would like to try some other ladies
with green eye shadow

I can't hold onto you
don't even want to
it's just my luck I'm programmed
to light up
at your face

but I'm tired of trying to play temptress
your monthly figure sounds reasonable

since you moved out it's been peaceful
I take Judy to school at eight
She's in an open classroom
She likes her teacher and the range of activities
Evenings friends come over
It's been surprisingly rejuvenating
I'm doing what I want with my life
no more compromises
         or psychodramas

Sometimes I have an ache
For one last response from you

But I tell myself
Forget that little itch
It's no longer part of moving on

I just wanted to say
I understand completely
your reasons for leaving
   you fat piece of shit
you're not as good-looking as you
                think you are.

Fifteen Years Ago, in the Park

It's happened to me,
lying in a woman's lap, that I saw
her face expand to meet the tree-tops,
her widening cheeks block out the sun,
her hair dazzled with gold leaf,
her frank green laughing eyes
turn uncertain
as though a cloud passed over them
while searching mine for an approving love.

I, her husband shrunk into her baby,
watched amazed and soundless as her face
eclipsed the universe, and almost giggled
at my helplessness, queasy
that this giantess looked at me for anything,
even, or especially, a simple kiss.

A Free Ride, New York

The black kids hanging on the backs of buses,
the passengers shocked inside:
"They'll get killed. Suppose a car
ploughed into the back, they'd be squashed!"
The black kids are grinning at the riders,
their intimacy both sinister and winning.
The passengers almost seem indignant
that nothing tragic's happening to the kids.
Finally, seeing a squad car approach,
the boys hop off.

You Were Afraid

you were afraid
we talked about it
then we went to sleep with the fan on

one of you turned and put your arm around me
another listened to the throbbing diesels
a third hid in the bathroom and cried
two out of three were alone

how little space our bodies fill in any room:
the deserted ceilings for instance
and the undersides of chairs where spiders think

the ledges in refrigerators
where dust collects around the light bulb
and while we sleep the hair grows in our nostrils

and while we sleep love disappears
like a shadow slipping under the door
leaving only a violet light to wonder at

Anger Showers

Under the shower
for half an hour
after our big fights:
the steam, the heat
had to beat it out of you—
the frustration at never
being able to make me see
how wrong I was, how
I distorted everything!

Once in a motel room,
when you wouldn't
let me touch you,
I insisted that you
never really loved me,
that your vanity alone
was wounded when I
wouldn't ask you to marry me,
and instead of saying
"You stupid idiot I did
love you and now I don't,"
you cried, "Oh I can't stand it!
You're trying to drive me crazy!"
and rushed into the shower.

Steam clouds whitened the room.
I waited for you to come out.
After twenty minutes I crept
into the bathroom, afraid
you were slitting your wrists
(projection: I'd been the
suicidal one) and feeling
like Norman Bates in *Psycho*,

spied on your lovely form against
the glass shower stall

When you finished at last
you swept by me, skin pink
and resilient, and cinched
an orange towel around your chest,
like Joan of Arc her breastplate:
"Don't say a word, I'll kill you
If you speak!" I spoke.
You ran out the door,
then returned, realizing
we were on a godforsaken highway
in Vermont. You'd have had
to hitchhike in your towel.
Scared you were mad enough to do it,
I promised to be silent.
You pulled a mattress on the floor,
very Japanese, like a futon,
for you to sleep alone.
The next day, all you said
By way of explanation was
"You like drama."

The Unexpected Failure

The show was bad, the child actors you directed
blew their lines. And yet you had
rehearsed them long enough.
You thought you could pull off a "light success."
The school audience was indulgent.
You counted all the things that could go wrong,
forgetting quite a few. By then it was
out of your hands, their own responsibility—
or was it yours, for trusting them too much?
But that was the point of your job:
you would take credit if they came through.
And they didn't; and you didn't.

The triumph you had so perfectly imagined,
even to the point of disdaining it,
would never leave the ideal realm of mind.
The hands stayed in the people's laps,
You heard them murmuring afterwards,
"Was that it?" And you hid.
Hid backstage, afraid and white,
Like bicarbonate of soda, waiting
to be pried open by a spoon.

You begged the feeling of shame to go away,
or else get worse. The pain inside your gut
demanded a knife to gouge out a cube of flesh,
a swift hard punch or something.
Superstitious placating of the Gods:
Failure, as always, made you think of God.
"He wants to slow you down," you smiled
at His futile tries
to teach you loss of ego.

Regrets

I never should have shaved off my moustache.
I wish I had married that rich widow.

All the time he was eating his whitefish platter,
I wanted a bite, yet said nothing.

I wanted to go to Mexico last summer;
I could have practiced my scuba diving.

For days I keep looking at my watch.
What's the matter with me, I can't get into the moment.

I went to see the world's greatest jazz musician.
After half an hour, I looked at my watch.

I don't relate to my astrological sign:
I feel it's imposed on me from without.

I've never admitted I don't like my nose.
Why give people the satisfaction?

The Little Magazines Keep Coming

The little magazines keep crawling under the door
like deformed hands on wheels
they can't help it if they whine and their paper skulls
are battered in by child-abuser mailmen
the little magazines keep coming

"I want my little magazine to be
a simple collection of poems,"
says one editor fastidiously,
so he asks everyone at a book party
to send him their poems,
and a year later he is sorry he began
but he must go to press
because he has a grant
from the Coordinating Council of Literary Magazines!

"It's not enough to print a nice array of poems"
he tells his wife while she sleeps in the middle of the night
"I must find some way to jazz it up.
Reviews, or photographs, those line drawings
at the bottom of the page…No, what I need is
a critical stance that will set the world of poetry right
and who cares if I make enemies?"

The little magazines come creeping under the door
like carnival freaks, half-men
unlovely but ambidextrous and hard to ignore.

Eunoch-unicorns, neglected progeny of monks and nuns
This one calls itself a Journal of Poetry and Protest
Another prints poems in comic strip form and asks
to be recycled.
Here's one that opens up like an accordion!

For awhile they have blue covers and chaste brown ink
or uncut pages, or play like audio cassettes

Offset or letterpress? The trudge to mimeo
Mimeo can look dignified in a pinch
though it's harder to collate
and where's the money for reams of paper
stamps manila envelopes the cover printed separately

and still to be won over the bookstore owners
with leathery faces like jaded degenerates' buttocks

Dog days—poverty and art—the shabby swollen gums
Baby's screaming wife's complaining but one is
taking the magazine to the printers!
At last, in that shirtsleeved inkstained machine-room
with piles of paper underfoot
discussing the layout with the printer
man-to-man
                    one can breathe

"I plan to give each poem its space to swim around in.
Tall, tall pages I'm thinking, with lots of white."

One editor is self-effacing, restricts his presence
to the Editor's Note. Another one decides:
"I'll print lots of my poems, so they'll know
what I stand for." A third scorns cliques and nepotism:
"No one has me in his pocket," he boasts like a candidate

Two friends, both magazine editors, have a quarrel
"Watch for my next issue!" snarls the first.
"How petty," thinks the second, "to use his journal for vendettas!"

Two friends, two spiders

But when you think of their blighted childhoods
And I beg you to think of his childhood for a moment
Ladies and gentlemen of the jury
when he daydreamed through chorus practice
that he would one day be great
and strike out twenty-seven batters in a row
Then the day came when he realized
he would never make the majors
that day when he began his literary career

So let tolerance have the final word
and let the little magazines come in,
for they are harmless
and can play in the corner if they want
so long as they don't get the rug wet with their drooling!

December

It was winter and the faces looked like raw beef,
the women's bodies pressed against their stiff coats,
their kidskin boots swam over their knees,
if you hung round museums long enough
you would run into someone you knew.
A sticking snow fell on the garbage can lids,
and on the green-tinted windows of city buses;
in the taxi a passenger was opening his mail
and slipping a gold wedding ring into his pocket.
A light snow had covered all our relationships,
but so fine the flakes that you no longer questioned
how to hold onto affection, allowing the sutures
to dissolve in the body, and I no longer cared
and I no longer cared if the snow in the gutter
turned to slush, releasing every friend from his vow,
and I no longer cared and was peaceful, like
a well-played clarinet in the hands of someone strong.
Crosstown bus, where are you taking me?

The Monster's Friends

I take out my collection of
Fights with best friends,
Those gaudy clashes that stay fresh,
Brighter than years of friendship.
Wooden soldiers fallen in battle,
I set them up before my eyes.
True, they quit on me first,
Yet few were traitors.
Most fled in horror, sensing
At last the enormity of the
Loyalty I demanded, the constancy,
Effort, depth of sympathy, belief,
While I reciprocated with
A disappointed smile.
They held out as long as they could,
Like a runner forcing his lungs—
Then suddenly took a slight
Lateral step, from one universe
To another. In surprise, they realized
They could live without my help,
Quite well, thank you, and breathe
Sharp clean air and expand
In the clear relief of their own ideas,
In a world without Phillip.
I, on the other hand, cannot live
In a world without Phillip
Because I *am* this thing,
This oppressive monster
That crushes and bullies all!

Secrets, Rehearsals

I waited for the deaths to deepen me.
My father, hanging on with dizzy spells,
my mother overweight, a likely stroke,
my sister Betty wandering in Asia—
how their deaths would slap me out of immaturity.
Still we were all together, Thanksgiving, alive.
I imagined a sorrow that rips us in half:
My brother Lenny stiff, my sister Joan run over.
Instead, all these piddling concerns
about "unsatisfied emotional needs."
I waited for life to turn tragic,
And then I would merely have to record it
to become a powerful, universal writer.

Sobbing in advance: at ten years old
I woke up from a dream in which I saw my father dead
And wrote a poem grieving at the vision.
My mother took it to her analyst,
He told her dreams were forms of wish-fulfillment.
She broke the hard news to me:
it wasn't that I loved my father so, but that
I wanted him dead to marry her.
This made no sense to me, but I
Am always willing to believe the worst,
And calmly accepted I might be harboring a parricide.

I must say, never for a conscious instant
did I wish my father dead, though often enough,
made eloquent by premature grief,
I have rehearsed Pop's funeral oration:
I'd ask that instead of the usual rigmarole
we could each say how we remembered him,
like the length of his neglected cigarette ash.
I would go first: rocking at the dais, *davening,*

trusting my stomach's churn to produce the right words,
I'd strike a balance between honesty and tact,
find meaning in a life where there seemed little.
But fuck all that! Let's talk truth now:
I never wished him dead, because
he was already half a corpse. Even his sarcasm
died long ago. What's left was phlegm.

When Mother called, I thought this must be it.
Instead, just one more sickness—pneumonia,
he needed to be taken to the hospital.
I came right over, glad that it was I
who had been called, depended on;
usually my older brother gets the call.
I helped Dad on with trousers, shirt,
knelt at his feet to strap on leather sandals
over phlebitis-swollen ankles. Something grand
about him then, the nobility of transit,
frail walker being lifted into cabs
in snow and ice, skimming the tricky sidewalks.

"He's always been a stoic," said my mother,
"so when he said he felt a little pain
I knew it must be bad. Poor Pop,
it hurt him so he's doubled over, couldn't
lie down, had to sleep all night in the chair.
I can't bear to see it happening to him.
He's like a great tree withering in its branches."

Come on. When was father ever a great tree?
Stoic, yes, freezing out pain and love;
once handed over to the admissions staff
he lost his grandeur, became a hospital thing,
whining about the food,
sunk in his bed-wetted trough
and over and over muttering, "Why me?"

As if you didn't know, you old possum.
Grey-stubbled, bone-protruding thin,
translucent as celery: "Don't worry, Pop,
tomorrow they'll give you a shave.
You'll look a million times better.
Why don't you put on your glasses?"
Nah, you don't wanna. You'd rather stare accusingly
at two feet of space in front of you.
You keep going on about those old outrages:
your Jewish rosary, memories of resentment
rubbed smooth by constant telling:
the time your rich, successful brother Arthur
said, running into you at a funeral,
"We are the only ones left. Let's be in touch.
Give me your phone number." And you replied
with offended dignity, "You know my phone number.
It's been in the book for years."

Of course *you* could have called him all those years.
Jacob and Esau, the same old junk.
A half-century ago, before your mother died,
Arthur, you claim, played up to her for a big wedding gift.
"He didn't care one bit about her, he was shamming.
He could make the tears roll down his eyes."
But you, you say with pride, were born close-mouthed,
could never be accused of sentimental gush.

Your children will attest to that.
Your oldest son can't forgive you for having been
so stingy to praise, so competitive at handball.
And I, Son No. 2, the poet, watch for apt details
as I have always done, a way to get through life:
the yellow plastic urine bottle you keep looking for.
"Gimme that thing," you point your bony finger
and keep it under the sheets, touching your groin.
The crotch and brain—as long as they're both attached

you're still alive; you hold onto your head,
afraid it'll come unscrewed and spin off
like a flying saucer around the room.
"What's wrong, Dad, got a headache?"
No, that's not it, you frown. I try to make
small talk. "What are the nurses like?
Find any sexually attractive?"
                              You look sternly at me,
the grey-green myopic eyes refusing rapport.
"Believe me, it's the most emasculating…
experience…imaginable," you say, swallowing slowly.

My sister Betty Ann, the family saint,
off seeking wisdom in Nepal, advises you to read
The Tibetan Book of the Dead
before it is too late. You're to summon the demons
before they leap on you; you're to look behind
the movie screen and realize all is shadow,
this World, this intravenous dripping…

Shadows like the amber traces oscillating
on the dark EKG screen, those jumps
more fascinating to me than any TV image,
which will it be, life, death?…while you go on
about how you impressed the nurses with
your big vocabulary, pride's last remnant.

My sister Joan, your youngest, wants something
from you before you go. A death-bed confession.
She wants to know where her father went.
She thinks she has the trump card
to make the frog's leg twitch a final time.
But all she'll get from you is more evasion:
"We made mistakes, sure. Nobody is perfect."
You built your life around avoiding life,
how could you be expected to stop now?

People don't grow nobler as they die,
don't scrap a lifetime of numbing habits
to sit up and tell truths.

And yet I keep on hoping you will tell me
something I don't know about The End.
We have been having these amazing skies
at sundown, the snow clouds pierced with
apocalyptic purple and red.
All New York can be seen from
your 16th story hospital room window.
Unfortunately, you won't put on your glasses
to look. You are saving your eyes, you say.
For what? I'd like to know.

"Do you want to hear the news?"
"What difference does it make?" you shrug.
"What have you been thinking all this time?"
"Nothing. When you're in pain,
that's all you think about is pain."
You blink your eyes to signal change of subject.
Is this, then, the illumination?

About the Author

Phillip Lopate was born in Brooklyn, New York in 1943, and received a BA from Columbia in 1964, and a doctorate from the Union Graduate School in 1979. After working with children for twelve years as a writer in the schools, he taught creative writing and literature at Fordham, Cooper Union, University of Houston, and New York University. He held the John Cranford Adams Chair at Hofstra University, taught in the MFA graduate programs at Columbia, the New School and Bennington., and is currently a Professor of Professional Practice at Columbia University.

He has written three personal essay collections — *Bachelorhood* (1981), *Against Joie de Vivre* (1989), and *Portrait of My Body* (1996); two novels, *Confessions of Summer* (1979) and *The Rug Merchant* (1987); two poetry collections, *The Eyes Don't Always Want to Stay Open* (1972) and *The Daily Round* (1976); a memoir of his teaching experiences, *Being With Children* (1975); a collection of his movie criticism, *Totally Tenderly Tragically*; an urbanist meditation, *Waterfront: A Journey Around Manhattan* (2004); and two biographical monographs, *Rudy Burckhardt: Photographer and Filmmaker* (2004) and *Notes on Sontag* (2009). In addition, there is a Phillip Lopate reader, *Getting Personal: Selected Writings* (2003).

He has edited the following anthologies: *The Art of the Personal Essay* (1994); *Writing New York* (1998), *Journey of a Living Experiment* (1979), *The Anchor Essay Annual* (1997–99), and *American Movie Critics* (2006). His essays, fiction, poetry, film and architectural criticism have appeared in many periodicals and anthologies.

He has been awarded a John Simon Guggenheim Fellowship, a New York Public Library Center for Scholars and Writers Fellowship, two National Endowment for the Arts grants, and two New York Foundation for the Arts grants.

Sandy McIntosh, *Ernesta, in the Style of the Flamenco*

Neil de la Flor, *Almost Dorothy*

Eileen Tabios, *The Thorn Rosary: Selected Prose Poems 1998–2010*

Paul Pines, *Last Call at the Tin Palace*

Edward Foster, *The Beginning of Sorrows*

Corinne Robins, *Facing it Again: New and Selected Poems*

Patricia Carlin, *Quantum Jitters*

Stephen Paul Miller, *Fort Dad*

Harriet Zinnes, *Light Light or the Curvature of the Earth*

Rochelle Ratner, *Ben Casey Days*

Jane Augustine, *A Woman's Guide to Mountain Climbing*

Thomas Fink, *Clarity*

Karin Randolph, *Either She Was*

Norman Finkelstein, *Passing Over*

Sandy McIntosh, *Forty-Nine Guaranteed Ways to Escape Death*

Eileen Tabios, *The Light Sang As It Left Your Eyes*

Claudia Carlson, *The Elephant House*

Steve Fellner, *Blind Date with Cavafy*

Basil King, *77 Beasts: Basil King's Bestiary*

Rochelle Ratner, *Balancing Acts*

Corinne Robins, *Today's Menu*

Mary Mackey, *Breaking the Fever*

Sigman Byrd, *Under the Wanderer's Star*

Edward Foster, *What He Ought To Know*

Sharon Olinka, *The Good City*

Harriet Zinnes, *Whither Nonstopping*

Sandy McIntosh, *The After-Death History of My Mother*

Eileen R. Tabios, *I Take Thee, English, for My Beloved*

Burt Kimmelman, *Somehow*

Stephen Paul Miller, *Skinny Eighth Avenue*

Jacquelyn Pope, *Watermark*

Jane Augustine, *Night Lights*

Thomas Fink, *After Taxes*

Martha King, *Imperfect Fit*

Susan Terris, *Natural Defenses*

Daniel Morris, *Bryce Passage*

Corinne Robins, *One Thousand Years*

Chard deNiord, *Sharp Golden Thorn*

Rochelle Ratner, *House and Home*

Basil King, *Mirage*

Sharon Dolin, *Serious Pink*

Madeline Tiger, *Birds of Sorrow and Joy*

Patricia Carlin, *Original Green*

Stephen Paul Miller, *The Bee Flies in May*

Edward Foster, *Mahrem: Things Men Should Do for Men*

Eileen R. Tabios, *Reproductions of the Empty Flagpole*

Harriet Zinnes, *Drawing on the Wall*

Thomas Fink, *Gossip: A Book of Poems*

Jane Augustine, *Arbor Vitae*

Sandy McIntosh, *Between Earth and Sky*

Burt Kimmelman and Fred Caruso, *The Pond at Cape May Point*

Marsh Hawk Press is committed to publishing poetry, especially to poetry with an affinity to the visual arts.

Artistic Advisory Board: Toi Derricotte, Denise Duhamel, Marilyn Hacker, Allan Kornblum, Maria Mazzioti Gillan, Alicia Ostriker, Marie Ponsot, David Shapiro, Nathaniel Tarn, Anne Waldman, and John Yau.

For more information, please go to: **http://www.marshhawkpress.org.**